Greatness is for Everyone

Everyone

The 4 traits of Greatness

BY CHARLES CHILDERS

authorHOUSE®

AuthorHouse™
1663 Liberty Drive
Bloomington, IN 47403
www.authorhouse.com
Phone: 1 (800) 839-8640

Published by AuthorHouse   02/21/2015

ISBN: 978-1-4969-6970-5 (sc)
ISBN: 978-1-4969-6969-9 (e)

Print information available on the last page.

Just what we want to hear:

"Thank you for a job well done." Or,
"I really appreciate the kindness and patience you showed me." Or,
"Your act of generosity helped me at a critical time in my life." Or,
"You are a great example for today's young people."

These are the words great people hear time and again as they go through the everyday encounters of life.

You and I can build lives of **_GREATNESS_**.
We can live by the 4 traits of **_GREATNESS._**

GREATNESS starts here and now.

Contents

**The last page is a copy of the Statement of Shared Values. This page may be reproduced and distributed as the need arises.

To Marsha Lynn, my wife, belongs the kudos for the comprehensibility and professionalism of my crude writing. Her expertise and patience with me and this work is testimony to her sterling character. Any errors of understanding or communication are all mine. To God belongs the glory.

Acknowledgements: Much of this book was written in the Fairfield Inn of Monument, CO. The customer service extended to my wife and me surpassed excellence. I was able to witness individuals living the *W—O—W—A* life. I want to thank personally Tami, Daniel, Shannon and of course, Katherine and Cheryl who made our lives comfortable and safe during a time of difficult transition in our lives.

Chapter 1

You And I Are Significant

While in kindergarten, I learned an important lesson regarding personal significance. I don't remember much about going to the carnival that day but a photograph was taken of me riding the roller coaster. This event was long ago probably near 1956, so the carnival ride was not one of the multi-story size that we see at amusement parks today. However, a newspaper reporter standing near the ride thought it interesting enough to take a picture of the riders. The next day my picture was in the local newspaper. My teacher, Mrs. Issacson, saw the picture, cut it out, and mounted it on the bulletin board with the caption "Who is this?"

Can you imagine the thrill in my young heart over the recognition? Perhaps her recognition explains why I can remember this minor event all these years later. That wonderful teacher on that day made me feel significant, not because of any innate special achievement or talent that I possessed. I was significant because of just being me. She merely recognized me and my significance.

Years later, I was in a discussion regarding the importance of the local newspaper. The presenter was arguing that community newspapers will always have their place in America because it is in the local newspaper that individuals can be publically recognized. Just today, I noticed the list of high school graduates in my hometown newspaper. This practice may have changed now in major cities, but I would still argue that recognizing individual significance is paramount to America's culture.

In the Bible, we read long lists of obscure names; i.e., Uzziah begat Jotham, Jotham begat Ahaz, and Ahaz begat Hezekiah and etc. Why all the names? We tend to skip through the Biblical genealogies. Why are the individual names specifically given? **It is because each individual is important to the story**. God doesn't make any insignificant people. No one is insignificant. God created you and me to be significant. Regardless of age, wealth, talent or lack thereof, or occupation or education, we are all significant with the potential to be great. Achievement is **not** the true, authoritative measure of significance. Each individual has the opportunity and the responsibility to utilize his/her freedom to cultivate ***GREATNESS*** from God given significance. The traits of personal ***GREATNESS*** are the same traits that our nation's founders envisioned as the foundation and perpetual objectives for America. Freedom or liberty is the political soil of ***GREATNESS***. The United States was uniquely created to maximize individual freedom.

Personal **GREATNESS** is the everyday demonstration of our God given, significance living under the power of morality. However mundane each day seems, as we act in freedom and with values our lives produce **GREATNESS**. Within America, we are great nationally when we together promote and protect the freedom of each individual to be great. **GREATNESS** is for everyone. We need not be the best at anything, possess the most of anything, or attain the highest in anything. We are great as we abide by the values of **GREATNESS**.

For example, meet Elias and Modesto, two great men who to this day speak to me of the priority of noble, personal values. I had the privilege to work beside them during my high school years on the golf course. They arrived at work every day at 4:30 a.m. so as not to be late for 6 o'clock. These men greeted their co-workers with joy and served their employer enthusiastically. Each man was an unsophisticated, honest, Hispanic man who personified **GREATNESS** for decades to their families and friends, of whom I was fortunate to be one.

What are the values of **GREATNESS**? Possible answers are youth, wealth, beauty, talent, fame, power, etc. If we now choose these values, then **GREATNESS** and significance are NOT for everyone. Only a few select people would ever be great and for most, their **GREATNESS** would be temporary at best. I suggest that more permanent and enriching values form personal **GREATNESS**.

These virtues are the basic building blocks of our individual **GREATNESS**. These virtues are expressed in the following four words and phrases:

3

Respect for __Work__,
>*Consideration of __Others__,*
>>*Appreciation of __True Wealth__, and*
>>*Submission to __Authority__,*

Also known as: *W—O—W—A.*

These four, personal values lived out in a nation protecting liberty and justice for all are the steps to GREATNESS.

It is no coincidence that the values of personal **GREATNESS** and the values that formed America are identical; we can call these values the American way.

America was built on a foundation of personal virtue or put another way personal values are the secret, indispensable ingredient for America and every individual. __*The fact is that personal GREATNESS and our nation's freedom are inseparably intertwined.*__ When America's fore-fathers planned, determined and wrote the Declaration of Independence, the Constitution, and the Bill of Rights, they envisioned a nation where citizens became the government and the government protected the citizens. Subsequently, the Federalists Papers were written and distributed defending and promoting this new nation and its ideals. The USA began with both written documents and with the unwritten code of the American way.

The magic for America is that free and moral men and women produce devoted families, prosperous businesses, and peaceful communities.

In America, the people and liberty are the paramount objective of the state. An authentic partnership exists between the people and the government. Therefore, we, the people and we, the leadership, are responsible to uphold the fundamentals of the tacit American way. The American way begins with the individual in our families, in our schools, and in our places of worship and then demonstrated through our government. What exactly is the American way?

Chapter 2

What Is The American Way?

The television announcer in 1961 begins,

> "The Adventures of Superman—*Faster than a speeding bullet! More powerful than a locomotive! Able to leap tall buildings at a single bound! Look up in the sky! It's a bird! It's a plane! It's Superman! Yes, it's Superman, strange visitor from another planet who came to Earth with powers and abilities far beyond those of mortal men. Superman, who can change the course of mighty rivers, bend steel in his bare hands; and who, disguised as Clark Kent, mild-mannered reporter for a great metropolitan newspaper, fights a never ending battle for truth, justice, and* __the American way__*."*

The American way is an undefined but clearly visible set of personal values that magnify the individual and unify us as a nation. Just as a good meal or an exotic dish includes the best ingredients combined in correct proportions and joined together under very specific mixing and cooking regimen. America is like a detailed recipe for a special entree including varied ingredients. America is the result of a social recipe: dedicated, educated, and religious men forming a new nation comprising a very diverse and independent population into a vision that offered peace, prosperity, and liberty to all. Our nation is not a casual, unpremeditated experiment without purpose or design. Rather America is solidly constructed upon principles and values drawn upon from history, philosophy, human nature, and from a divine design. Understanding our origin is essential to explain the foundation of America's past success, and our values also point the way to our *GREATNESS*.

Freedom demands a population that collectively upholds specific, but unwritten national principles, priorities, and values. These values at one time formed a core within America. This moral core is the American way. The truth is that personal, moral values defined America. Our nation has been husbanded into existence by its values, by the American way.

The American way is a set of personal values woven into our nation, a nation committed to liberty and justice for all. The American way defined our nation more so than any particular ethnicity or language. Individuals and families travelled from all over the world; we desired freedom and we came to understand the power of moral virtue within a democracy. Personal values were and are the gold and precious stones of the American culture.

The values were practiced by teachers, bankers, farmers, craftsmen, family members, and even politicians.

Virtues were translated into a commitment for a new nation and a commitment to freedom.

In the Preamble to America's Constitution, we read *"We the People of the United States, in Order to form a more perfect Union, establish Justice, insure domestic Tranquility, provide for the common defence, promote the general Welfare, and secure the Blessings of Liberty to ourselves and our Posterity, do ordain and establish this Constitution for the United States of America."*

The plain inference is that in America, the people formed a more perfect Union in order to protect the significance (Justice, Tranquility, and general Welfare) of each individual. In America, **the people** are more valuable, more sacred, and more significant than the government.

Unlike most nations where power is worshipped, America was formed to maximize the freedom and uniqueness of the individual over the image of the state. The objective was to promote individual freedom, rights, and responsibilities. **The USA is the societal outgrowth of the belief that everyone is significant and that everyone must be proactively self-responsible.** Personal significance and self-reliance are at the cellular level of the American way. However short of our ideals America has been and is, we must never stop our pursuit of the enduring values of ***GREATNESS*** for the individual. The American way builds ***GREATNESS***.

Let me repeat: ***The magic for America is that free and moral men and women produce devoted families, prosperous businesses, and peaceful communities***. Excessively dominant governments do not produce harmonious communities, successful businesses, kind hearted families, or good men and women

An unwritten partnership exists between America and her citizens. This partnership is now sorely misunderstood and abused. This social contract between the USA and Americans is extraordinarily generous with freedom, historically unique in citizen participation, and monstrously demanding in responsibilities. The founding fathers understood this interdependent relationship and were willing to die in order to give birth to America and to the American way of life. Men and women through two centuries have also understood and prized this country for this relationship. Today, Americans must understand the philosophic basis of a democratic America and accept the responsibilities of a free America.

This partnership is described simply as freedom from political domination in exchange for personal, self-control. America has provided freedom for over 240 years and has always needed restraint and responsibility from the citizenry. We will maintain a GREAT nation as long as the people live GREAT lives. The nation will protect and nourish liberty as long as the people live and preserve morality. Once morality collapses, America will suffer. America both provides the environment to her citizens for GREATNESS and demands GREATNESS from its citizens. The lifestyle that leads to personal ***GREATNESS*** is called the American way.

A conversation must begin between you and me and throughout America. The question is "What kind of people and what kind of nation do we want?" Do we want to change our values? Will we remain free and prosperous if we do change our values? Do we want the judges, the politicians, and the super-wealthy to control us? Will we let small minorities dictate policy decisions? We, the people, deserve wiser and nobler leadership and decision making.

The following diagrams are an attempt to drive home the relationship between the individual and the nation within the United States. The top image has the individual in the center with concentric circles of influence benefitting from the moral choices of the individual lives. In this diagram, the focus is on the contribution the individual performs from the inside the social network outward. The social network begins with the individual into and through families, communities, and society at large within the nation. The background is the personal, moral values of **WORK**, **OTHERS**, **WEALTH**, and **AUTHORITY** on which America is built. A free society cannot function successfully without the individual and the social network providing the moral foundation of a workable democracy.

The bottom diagram is no less important if the individual is going to reach his/her fullest productivity. The USA is in the center with the concentric circles of the social building blocks comprising a free society. The nation working through the state and local communities and the family provides the protective and positive environment for the individual. The governments can do much to facilitate the contributions of individual and the benefits to the individual in a social network. All the circles of the social network and the individual are positioned in the background of opportunities for **Freedom**, **Peace**, **Prosperity**, and **Happiness**.

The Role of the Individual

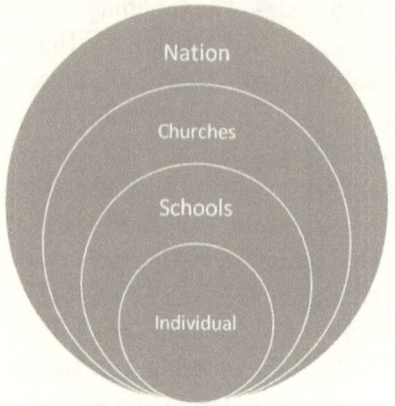

Shared Responsibilities of ***Work, Others, Wealth, and Authority***

The Role of the Nation

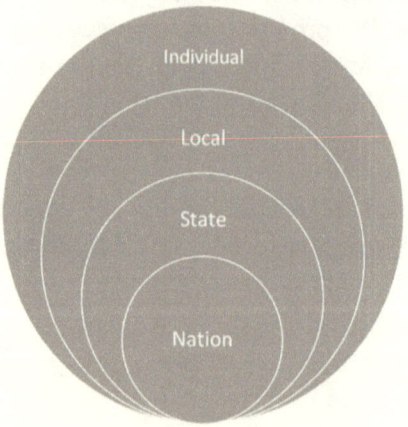

Opportunities for ***Freedom, Peace, Prosperity, and Happiness***

America was deliberately and prudently designed with this social contract between the individual and the nation in mind. Presently, both parties of this contract are failing. The morality of individuals is crumbling and the performance of the government is failing. The social contract for America is being overwritten with ideas that will fail. We can reach upwards to the American way of **GREATNESS. _Let's run after GREATNESS._**

America has been built by four very specialized institutions. These institutions should be thought of as four functional units of one organization. These units are as follows: the family, schools, churches, and government. Just like a football team has an offensive unit and a distinct defensive unit, **GREATNESS** in America is built by the efforts of each of the four units. Each of the four functional units builds an ingredient into the **GREATNESS** of the individual and the nation.

For example, the family teaches the individual how to be civil, courteous, and respectful. We are taught the value of others and how to relate to others in cooperation and enjoyment. Schools prepare us for work and our lifelong pursuits of creativity. Churches teach us the value of non-materialism, the value of generosity, and the meaning our lives can find. And government teaches us the value of unity through the respect for law and respect for those who serve the law.

A chart depicting these functional units and their results is as follows:

Unit:	GREATNESS:	Lessons:	Results:
Family	Others	Civility	Cooperation
Schools	Work	Creativity	Production
Churches	Wealth	Charity	Donation
Government	Authority	Country	Nation

GREATNESS for the individual and for the nation is built by the lessons learned from and the contributions of each functional unit to the whole. Imagine a nation lacking any of these ingredients. We cannot allow these four functional units to fall into disrepair.

Do not think of these four as arbitrary institutions. These units are the brick layers, the construction workers, and the foremen building great individuals and a great nation. America has been built brick by brick or individual by individual through the vigorous efforts of each unit.

Certainly, the roles are not rigidly distinct from each other. Rather they are complementary. Just as in football, the defensive unit can score a touchdown by recovering a fumble and advancing it for a touchdown, so too these cultural units can and will complement the work performed by the other units of society.

However, today too many failures in each unit are being magnified by the compounding failures of the other units. Marriage vows and families are ending in divorce and being bypassed altogether in birthing children and attempting to raise them to maturity. Schools are failing to produce willing and able workers leaving too many without the skills necessary to succeed in our complex and competitive world. Churches are not teaching noble values but philosophy, sociology, and psychology in the place of spiritual values and truth. Our government has missed the mark for which it was designed and is meddling in far too many, wrongheaded areas of society.

America must rediscover the family, the school, the church or synagogue, and the government into the functional areas for which each was designed. The heroes in a great America are the two parent families, the school teachers, the church and synagogue pastors, and the policemen who every day pass on the enriching values that make America great. The lessons of **WORK. OTHERS, WEALTH, AND AUTHORITY** are infinitely important and irreplaceable to **GREATNESS,** Freedom, and Justice in America.

Chapter 3

How Greatness Is Achieved.

GREATNESS is achieved through the moral exercise of the talents, responsibilities, and opportunities endowed upon each individual by God. **GREATNESS** is being all that we can be and being all that God has designed us to be. The United States is great as it protects the environment for personal advancement for ALL of its citizens to reach for his/her individual **GREATNESS**.

How do we, individually and nationally, identify personal significance and produce **GREATNESS**? How can our nation, the United States of America, be great or successful in fulfilling its ideals? History suggests that America has demonstrated signs of greatness from its earliest years. God has blessed America with peace and with prosperity in a measure not equaled by other nations. However, at times, America has failed to be great; an example is our need to fight the Civil War to end the evil of slavery. And, this present day too, we are falling below our potential to be a great people and a great nation.

In our debate over change, we must not lose America's magic, purpose, and design. We must not lose the values that made America great. We are currently pursuing paths of moral confusion and political misdirection; we are corrupting our values. **_W—O—W—A_** is a description of the American way and a path to **_GREATNESS_**. The good news is that tens of millions of Americans already subscribe to these noble values. America has a rich foundation of honorable citizens, i.e. Elias and Modesto. America, while not at all perfect, is a GREAT nation with GREAT people, but we are altering our values and **not** in ways or paths that will produce continued freedom and **GREATNESS**. Let me explain how my thoughts have developed.

I have spent many delightful moments and hours observing and enjoying my canine friends. These special dogs are examples of values driven living. These friends helped me to think positively about America's future because they helped me to understand **_GREATNESS_** and the power of values driven living—living consistent with **_W—O—W—A_** values.

Let me introduce Crystal, my first girlfriend after divorce; I was starting my adult life for the second time. She was a sheltie mix, a puppy when we first met. Crystal was the love of my life; she returned to me my sense of receiving love again. She overwhelmed with the knowledge that personal significance is important and that small gestures of recognition can dramatize this importance. She was always excited to see me and I to see her.

After meeting and marrying Marsha Lynn, Lili was adopted into our family of two adults, five kids, and, of course, Crystal. Lili was a tiny beagle pup with an adorable wrinkled face and brown eyes that could turn any heart.

And through the years came, Andi and Max and then Foxworth, a large black Newfoundland. Andi, a golden retriever, joined our family during our evacuation from New Orleans and Hurricane Andrew, hence her name. Max was a muscular Rottweiler, a powerful dog, able to be both frightening and loving depending on the relationship to him. Our large dogs protected us and motivated us to think of others always and of their needs.

As I began writing this manuscript, Foxworth was my walking partner. But I mustn't forget Mr. Bojangles, a Shih Tzu, who was our inside companion. Sadly, after many wonderful years, these great companions have all passed.

Why was their companionship important? As we walked and watched and sniffed, I prayed. I prayed that God would teach me: Right from wrong—Best from merely good—Peace through the storms—Guidance through the darkness—Right choices in innumerable situations.

Sometimes the dogs and I stopped along the way to listen and watch. I wanted to hear, observe, think, learn, and enjoy God's fellowship. He revealed Himself to me in fresh ways with spiritual perspectives. Often, while my friends were relaxing and wandering about, God was gripping me with His nature, truth, wisdom, and power.

He was reminding me of Bible verses that I have read and prayers that I have prayed throughout the years.

During our walks, I was trying to understand and apply my Christian faith to my personal hopes and plans and the practical concerns of my wife, my work, my children, finances and more. My friends and I wrestled with understanding and applying biblical principles to modern life in America. How do the issues of my life fit together? How can I be a better husband, dad, and business manager? And, on behalf of our country, how can the nation I love solve its 21st century issues?

Furthermore, I wondered what made America great in the past and if we are losing our *GREATNESS* as individuals and as a nation today? I think we are; and I have concluded that ***the answer lies within you and me as citizens*** and only secondarily in Washington, D.C. I believe America's *GREATNESS* is built upon a powerful set of both personal and commonly shared values. I define the four values that have built and guided our nation into prosperity as *Work*, *Others*, *Wealth*, and *Authority* or *W—O—W—A*, for short.

Honorable, moral values built a GREAT people and a GREAT nation. In their absence or in their abuse, *GREATNESS* can and will slip away. With the loss of personal and national *GREATNESS*, the peace, prosperity, freedom, and security we have enjoyed will suffer.

Chapter *4*

Bo Was A Great Little Dog

Mr. Bojangles, Bo, was a small Shih Tzu, literally translated from Chinese meaning "lion dog." Shih Tzus are depicted throughout Chinese and Tibetan art to resemble the lion in appearance.

Whatever the physical resemblance and size difference, Bo was GREAT because of his heart. He could be stubborn when he is pulling at his leash with all of his 15 lbs. He could be aggressive and noisy especially when another dog approached regardless of the size of this new opponent. But most of the time he was affectionate, companionable, and loyal. If I wanted to read, he sat by my feet. If I was ill, he lay in bed beside me. If I wanted to walk or go on an errand in the car or even ride the motorcycle, Bo was eager to be with me.

He wouldn't let us forget his biscuits in the morning and his treats throughout the day. Bo required a short walk in the morning and another in the cool of the evening. He was a small, but a GREAT dog.

Bo defined **GREATNESS** by giving from his heart, serving, and being friendly to all. He never met a stranger that he didn't love. We joked in our house when we said to Bo, "Please go get my glasses." He jumped up and stood on his toes and trembled with excitement. He was after the requested item. He may not know where to look, and he may not have the thumbs necessary to grasp the object, but he was ready. He never conveyed (like I might), "Can't you see I am napping now. Go; get it yourself." or "You dummy, are you making fun of my inability to grasp onto things?" No, for Bo, serving, being a companion, listening, and responding with a grin and a wagging tail were his signs of **GREATNESS**.

I know that most have or have had a dog like Bo. Aren't these companion pups wonderful? Yes, a thousand times; we need more dogs like him. We also need people like him.

How can Americans, you and I, adopt this lifestyle of **GREATNESS**? We can be unselfish, kind, giving, patient, preferring others above ourselves. We can be loyal, honest, good friends, attentive listeners, and loving spouses. We can prefer serving others to being served. We can choose honorable values.

Americans can choose to be great by choosing right values, honorable traits, and godly virtues. I am very much a work in process. I am a fallen person; however, I can choose to be great on a daily basis. **GREATNESS** is found in the heart and demonstrated through the values by which we live. **GREATNESS** is not synonymous with being the "greatest." Some try to be the greatest athletes, businessmen, or politicians. The pursuit of being the greatest or the richest or the most powerful or the most known can lead us into the immorality of winning at all costs even at the compromise of our character. However, personal ***GREATNESS*** is not in competition with anyone else; ***GREATNESS*** is adopting and practicing the higher values of life. Bo was not drawn into the vanities of being the "greatest"; his life's goal was to be great in pleasing and serving me.

How do we perform our jobs? How attentive are we at home? How patient are we with ourselves and others? Great people will fail at times with our tasks even as Bo did. Great people may be bested by others. But, the power of ***GREATNESS*** is in serving, giving, sharing, listening, loving, obeying, and not in always being the first or the best or the most at anything. ***GREATNESS*** is measured in what we value and in our commitment to live by those values.

Bo knew the meaning of ***GREATNESS***. He accepted his limitations and gloried in his strengths. He was not Max, or Andi, or Foxworth. He admired the other dogs in our family, but he was content being the "little buddy" with the great heart. His heart weighed less than a pound but its strength could carry our entire family. ***GREATNESS*** is found in the values of the heart.

All of us want and hope to be remembered with honor. We want an honorable legacy or to be remembered for being great people. Very few of us will have the talent or the fame to be remembered. A much smaller percentage will be remembered with fondness. However, we can all choose the life values that will create ***GREATNESS***.

We can choose great values. We as individuals and as a nation can be GREAT if we choose the values that lead in the right direction. We choose the values that define our lives. Personal significance is a gift from God; however, individual and national *GREATNESS* **is the product of the values and the moral choices we make.**

I repeat again: *The magic for America is that free and moral men and women produce devoted families, prosperous businesses, and peaceful communities.* I believe in this magic. If we have lost some of this magic, we can get it back. Free and moral people can build a great and productive nation.

Actions are the universal words of *GREATNESS*. Without raising voices and even without a drum roll, actions say to the world "I am somebody of great significance." Bo never said a word and rarely barked but his joy, spirit, and love filled our home with the glory of his significance. People noticed him, praised him, and paid him special attention. His actions were an enthusiastic greeting, a warm kiss, an unselfish heart, and respectful silence when others were talking. These actions spoke without words and communicated in a universal love language. We can learn this language; we can adopt the four principles of *GREATNESS*.

Chapter 5

Understand The Uniqueness Of America?

Think of the United States of America as an experiment in human relations. Whether we choose to participate or not, you and I are in this experiment. We are being tested psychologically, socially, politically, and legally. The thesis being tested is: ***Can free men and women govern themselves especially over the long term?***

The question is not whether freedom is good for mankind. We know that the human heart needs liberty and flourishes in freedom. The problem with freedom is that it can be spoiled by internal, moral confusion and then dominated by external, forceful control. Therefore, freedom must be continually inoculated against moral corruption. The results of moral decay are social, economic, and political corruptions; these corruptions drift into cultural and political anarchy. This anarchy weakens the culture until freedom is surrendered to excessive, elitist control. Freedom can mistakenly condone moral license for any and all behaviors even behaviors that are not healthy, productive, or wise. Political anarchy is the result of this moral confusion; citizens and the government cannot determine right from wrong. Moral confusion ultimately results in political gridlock where cooperation and problem solving within a society cease to exist. Problems will then accumulate causing dissatisfaction and disunity within the society leaving that society an easy prey for political domination.

When problems cannot be solved, one group or the other will try to solve the unavoidable conflicts of self-interest by deception and/or force. Freedom must be protected from internal, moral corruption and from the resulting political confusion. Freedom is not the problem; the long term implementation of freedom is the challenge. The USA was designed to minimize the disruptive habits of mankind and yet to maximize personal freedom. The question is **can we govern ourselves rightly in order to maintain freedom without moral decline?**

The experiment is psychological because it asks the question: What do Americans claim are their individual rights and individual responsibilities? Our answers are conveyed in every word and action that flows from our lives. Can I govern myself to make good choices? Will I control my base nature and mature into a productive adult? Am I confident enough in myself to support myself and to live peaceably with others?

But more than one level of testing exists; we are also tested socially. What do I think about other American citizens, their rights, and their responsibilities to me? For example, when I drive my car and I need to make room for others, what do I think about their schedules and their safety? Am I responsible to my brothers in America? The questions come at us fast and furiously. We have no time to think or is it that we don't want to think about anyone but ourselves. How are we doing socially?

We are also tested politically. Can we find mutually beneficial solutions in a peaceful and quiet manner? Politics is the occupation of finding the best, workable solutions for all concerned. We can disagree but can we solve issues among equals without having to pull the power trigger? Whether we use words, guns, or the voting booth, the test is: Can we work together to find political solutions to difficult issues without force, deception, or bribery? Can we minimize differences and maximize statesmanship, the art of compromise and cooperation over disagreement and disunity?

Lastly, we are being tested legally. Will we obey the laws of the land? Our US Constitution and The Bill of Rights are just the beginning of the laws written by elected representatives to protect our freedom. Our military protects freedom from outside intrusion and our legal system serves to protect freedoms from internal corruption. The test is: Will we adjudicate the law to uphold morality or denigrate the law to the whim of every social upheaval? Will we obey the laws or undermine them for selfish gain? Will we influence the law for personal benefit at the expense or loss of freedom for others?

If Americans do well on these four tests, then our nation has nothing to fear in the future. Freedom can and will overcome the external adversaries and the internal conflicts, if we choose right values. We will continue to be a **GREAT** nation pointing other nations to freedom, if we choose rightly. **<u>But what if we don't?</u>**

So how are we doing on these tests? Give yourself and the rest of us a grade. Pass or Fail? Psychologically? Socially? Politically? Legally? History records that we have achieved some great cultural advancements, i.e., over 230 years of democracy. However, we are at a crossroads right now. Quite literally, this generation of Americans is deciding anew what personal values and what national values we desire for ourselves and for the next generations. We are changing our values at this very moment.

Psychologically, we are focused more on personal pleasure than on personal responsibility. Socially, we arming ourselves for protection against one another rather than living at peace with or serving our neighbors. Our families are disintegrating as we watch more television and movies preoccupied with violence and immorality. Politically, we are fast becoming a nation of the powerful controlling the freedoms of the people, leaving the people confused, disengaged, and distrustful of our country's government. Presently, we are legalizing new moral freedoms that previous generations rejected, and we are resisting all forms of authority from parental to social and legal. Our nation is changing. Can we change so fundamentally and still flourish as individuals and as a nation?

The founding fathers of America believed freedom could be entrusted to a democracy, well stated by Abraham Lincoln as "a government of the people, by the people, and for the people." We, the people, must answer the question: What is the essential foundation for our freedom and for our democratic republic? The framers of the US Constitution had the benefit of many respected and established philosophers on the subject of freedom and government. A new nation won its independence and formed its new government founded upon the conclusions of centuries of political thought. Underlying our nation are the carefully studied principles of morality, justice, and freedom. America was built upon a foundation of unwritten, personal values and priorities that could be called the "American Way." Our US Constitution recognizes the power in the people to govern themselves rightly. We have the power to govern, but do we have the wisdom to choose rightly and the self-control to govern rightly? Is the American way the way of the future?

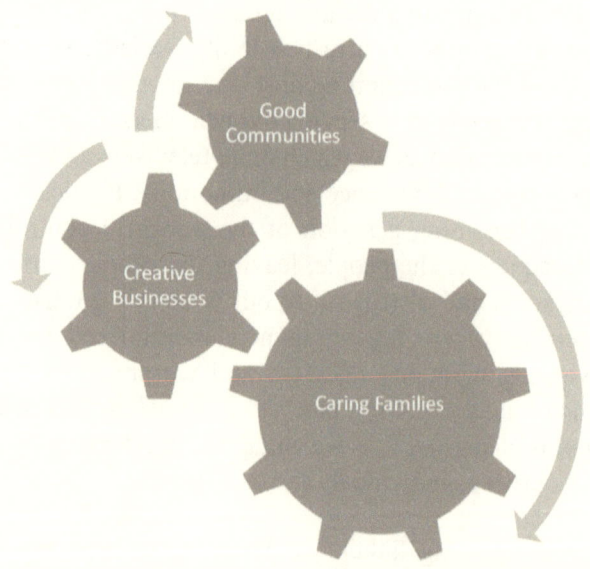

The magic for America is that free and moral men and women produce devoted families, prosperous businesses, and peaceful communities. You and I are the power and genius behind a great America. Free and moral people can produce a great and productive nation.

Chapter 6

Is The American Way Relevant To 21ˢᵗ Century America?

In order to understand the importance of the American way, America must review the original purpose and design for our country.

According to the Declaration of Independence, America's purpose is to promote greater God-given, human fulfillment through increased personal freedoms and responsibilities protected by a limited national government. The United States of America exists to protect and facilitate the individual and the God endowed individual pursuits of life, liberty, and happiness.

<u>*The fundamental equations for the United States are:*</u>

Personal Values + Individual Freedom
= *the American Way of Life*

and

The American Way of Life + Limited
Government = the U.S.A.

The American way of life is **first** a set of moral, personal values combined with abundant personal freedom. In America, each individual is encouraged to pursue his/her ambitions and goals within the bounds of a personal value system which include morality, justice, and fairness for others. A personal value system is ***essential*** to freedom and to America. When personal freedom is exercised without moral values, confusion and gridlock paralyze society. This condition helps to explain the state of gridlock within American politics today. If Americans are redefining and changing our values, then our nation can lose its moral compass and fall into moral confusion and political paralysis.

By far, the most effective problem solving society is a values driven citizenry combined with a limited government. National government is necessary to protect the freedoms of the citizenry from internal and external elitist control. However, this government must be limited to the role of protection from intrusion, not superiority over the individual rights to choose nor the financial provision for the people. When government insists on overreaching or attempts the wrong functions, freedoms are lost and government's effectiveness is diminished. When individuals are content and even insistent that government provide for them the basic sustenance of food, health, and income, then those very individuals are pushing government beyond the original design of our forefathers. Pushing government to fulfill roles for which it was not designed will fail.

Today America is battling between two errors: the confusion of lowered personal values and the futile attempts of an expanded national government. Neither lowered values nor expanded government will make America GREAT.

We can be and will be most proud of Americans and of America when liberty for all is combined with the American way of personal values and a limited national government. Then, Americans will be busy creating and producing the fruit of their labors. Increased individual freedom under the influence of responsible men and women is the formula of the United States and the American way. *GREATNESS* will only result in a society where freedom, personal values, and limited government are functioning, each within its scope and limits.

If America is to remain free and produce great results, then we as a people must return to the personal values that once defined individuals living in America and that can define us again. Also, the American government must be forced back into its appropriate role of safe-guarding the public. Neither over-regulating public policy nor being the rich benefactor for the people will reach our American goals.

America can forfeit its claim to ***GREATNESS*** and freedom through the combined **losses of personal values** and through the mis-application of an **over-zealous government**. Without values, America is mired in moral confusion not discerning right from wrong. Under the power of an amoral population and a misguided government, we as Americans can be trapped in the manipulation of the political and/or economic elite. Wealthy, politically powerful, and socially connected elite will dominate a society weakened by immorality. We, as individuals and as a nation, can lose our ***GREATNESS*** through the errors we are now choosing, and then we will lose our productivity, unity, and freedom.

In all we do as 21st century Americans, citizens must practice the values that make both the individual and America **G R E A T**. Excessive moral freedom and excessive government control are a recipe for failure, the opposite of our original recipe for America. Our moral choices determine our future.

Chapter 7

Learning To Walk Without The Leash

Learning to walk off leash is every dog's challenge and opportunity. Walking off leash is never easy; I have had dogs that met the challenge and others that never did. My custom is to walk with my dog every morning at about 6:00 a.m. for 30-45 minutes before work and on the weekends. This walk is an opportune time to think, pray, make decisions and enjoy the beauty God has given to us. Also, after dinner between 8-9 pm, my dog and I go out again to relax and rest in preparation for a night's sleep.

This schedule has been my habit with my walking companions, most recently Foxworth, but before Crystal, Andi, and Max. We have walked in neighborhoods, in country settings, in dog parks and just about anywhere we found ourselves. We have always used a leash because this physical connection affords safety for the dog and a tug at me if I move too slowly.

When in the country or in a fenced park, I might unleash the safety line between my friend and me. The results are interesting. Max, my Rottweiler ran around but he always kept his eye on me and returned by voice command or even a wave, if I wanted him. I could trust him. However, Crystal never did learn to stay near me. She ran off immediately; she might look back at me as if saying, "Catch me, if you can!" She was the sheltie mix; her nature was to run and run for a very long time. I often had to break off the walk and retrieve her, usually not in the best of moods.

With Foxworth, my Newfoundland, I used a high tension rope and my phone number was embroidered on his collar. We walked in a rural neighborhood, and he craved the hint of freedom. He too, if given the chance ran away and was lost away from home. Fortunately however, he was rescued and later returned to me by other dog lovers before tragedy struck.

As American citizens, our invisible leashes are the values of right living. The values we hold as important become the motivations and the guidelines for our behaviors in every social interaction from marriage to business to government.

Integrity is the internal leash that enables the machinery of a society to function. ***Honesty is the super principle upon which all other moral values depend.*** When a man or a government says what it means and means what it says, trust forms between man to man, business to consumer, and government to the people. When a person is honest both in private and in public, others can trust him or her. All human relationships demand honesty; honesty creates trust. Integrity is more critical to a society than the law. Integrity inspires virtue; virtue leads to right behavior and behaviors produce acts of kindness, creativity, and nobility. Dishonesty on any and all levels is always destructive.

Moral principles are the guide rails for decision making and conduct. Principles based on our values are the road signs that enable us to make the right decision when tempted to do otherwise. Do we run off-leash with what feels good, what seems good, or do we remain true to our guiding principles and values?

Each decision we make is governed by a combination of passion, pragmatism, or principles (values). Our decisions and actions must be overwhelmingly governed by honorable principles lived out with integrity, not our passions or even our pragmatism.

Can we trust one another to make decisions through the free exercise of our noble values for the benefit of all concerned? Free exercise is the freedom from external restraints **but not the absence** of the internal restraints of morality, integrity, and conscience.

Sadly, Foxworth and Crystal are examples of lives mis-guided by instincts, smells, and curiosity. A smell, another animal, or a bright color attracted them and without thought to principles or especially to consequences, they ran with all their might. If they happened to be off leash, the results could have been frightening. As a result, their freedom was always limited by the leash, a safety device.

However, Max was very unique; he considered me his guiding principle. Like all dogs he loved the smells and attractions of all varieties. But Max always stayed close regardless of the tempting distraction. I could walk him at night in the park near the river, and he was close. At other times, he might wander further away chasing a provocative attraction, but never so far that he couldn't see me and return. Of course, this controlled walk took some training; he was not always obedient. But as he matured, he earned more and more freedom or time off leash.

I define maturity as learning to live by values rather than by instincts, desires, or outside restraints, i.e. the leash. As we mature, we can be trusted to make decisions guided by the highest and best values. In doing so, we gain the most freedom. Living by right values prevents costly mistakes and affords us the highest freedom. Presently in America we have freedom; however, we must not use our freedom to lower our values. The positive result of freedom plus virtue is ***GREATNESS***, both individually and nationally. The personal values are: ***Work***, ***Others***, ***Wealth***, and ***Authority***. The acronym is ***W—O—W—A***.

A values driven life does not condemn others. The worst life lived is the life of self-righteousness. Jesus responded to the woman caught I adultery with compassion and to the Pharisees with correction, "He who is without sin should throw the first stone." He also said in another context, "First, take the log out of your own eye." We must apply personal values to our own lives and then, stand with others heart to heart in reinforcing right behavior. We need each other's help not each other's criticism for poor behavior nor approval when we are actually behaving badly.

A healthy society does not lower values so that every behavior is comfortable, rather, a good culture will lift, love, and pray for each other. A society requires shared values not forced or coerced values. Shared, moral values will pinch each of us from time to time; we can encourage one another and challenge one another to grow up together into maturity. Thomas Jefferson wrote that in America "the law is King" in obvious opposition to the capriciousness of the King of England. The law has always and will continue to legislate morality, however, if the personal morality has imploded, then the legislative morality will fail.

A wise man once said "God loves us just as we are, but He loves us too much to leave us there." No truer words have ever been said. Mankind is not abandoned to wander and scrounge like an unloved and lost dog. God is not the critical coach demanding that we jump higher and run faster. Nor is He the grumpy boss pushing for more work and offering less reward. Rather He is more like the mom seeking the lost coin, the shepherd chasing after the wandered lamb, and the dad rejoicing over the rebellious, but returning son. God is not demanding what He has not provided. He is both the One who defines right living and the One who enables living rightly. He is the good and wise Shepherd, loving, forgiving, guiding, nourishing, and strengthening. God doesn't make junk; we are all in His heart of love.

Chapter 8

W—O—W—A Values

Before we think together about each principle one at a time, let's consider a statement of shared values, *W—O—W—A*. Nearly every U.S. citizen I meet believes that America is on the wrong path. I suggest that if we adopt this statement of shared values, we can change our misdirection and safeguard our freedoms. We, the people, and we, the leadership of America, can learn this statement and live out the values stated below:

Statement of Shared Values

We thank you, God, for the endless blessings of freedom and we joyfully assume responsibility for maintaining our freedom.

We hereby affirm these statements of shared responsibilities.

*Our government must never promise to do for us what we must do for ourselves. And, we must never ask our government to give to us what we must earn through **work**.*

*Our nation was commissioned by God to protect and enable the rights of everyone in a concerned and compassionate community. Our personal worth is found in serving **others**.*

*Our relationships and our personal character traits are the measures of real and lasting **wealth**. Family is our greatest asset and our most important gift to the future.*

*Our peaceful society depends on the adherence by all to the laws of the land. If the law is to be changed, it is through public debate and submission to divine **authority**.*

Therefore, we believe that freedom is an earned right. <u>This right can be lost if not honored and upheld.</u> The responsibility is mine.

So help me, God. <u>(My signature goes here.)</u>

In a democracy, the people vote not just with their ballot but with their life choices. We, the people, are America—more than any party, leader, or issue. What does the United States stand for in this modern age? We select our work, our way of treating others, our pursuit of wealth and power, and our respect for the law.

What if, for example, investors guided the financial decisions through the W—O—W—A school of investment philosophy?

Investment decisions would not be the passive and computer controlled procedures of today's financial markets. Investors would examine businesses looking for long term product innovation, management and employee creativity and stability, and reachable growth possibilities in the industry. Investors would put their money into people and ideas not into financial weapons of computer trading and arbitrage profiteering. Why? The goal is only partly personal gain but also the gain for business owners, employees, the community, and the nation. These are not new ideas or investment strategies. Investment in promising products and creative entrepreneurs is the original intent of Wall Street.

The American economy within a moral system focuses on building the better widget, designing practical solutions to everyday tasks. America is spending its wealth gaining more wealth for some but not producing better quality answers to the needs of its citizens. Modern America is similar to the man in the New Testament who built bigger barns rather than feeding the hungry or teaching others how to feed themselves. This rich man was to learn that financial wealth does not enrich the soul. Jesus was not impressed by this man's wealth.

Morality will have similar effects in every aspect of human endeavor. Teachers would teach and be role models for their students. America would lead the world with unselfish statesmanship; leaders would serve the nation not their position or wealth. Workers would work with skill and diligence. Employees would serve with dependability and industry. Men with money would seek to do good for others. And, authority would be obeyed with respect and trust. Personal and national morality opens doors to problems solved, solutions found, and answers created. Families would stay together; this social pattern alone would change America.

Chapter 9

On The 4ᵗʰ Of July, 2014

We thank you, God, for the endless blessings of freedom and we joyfully assume responsibility for maintaining our freedom.

On the 4ᵗʰ of July, I was having lunch with Bailey, my nine year old grandson; we were discussing the reason for celebrating. We talked about the Declaration of Independence, the Revolutionary War, and the historic heroes of George Washington and Thomas Jefferson. Of course, we talked about fireworks and the reminder the loud explosions and bright, colorful flashes are to us that our nation and freedom had to be won in a fiery battleground.

During our conversation, Bailey said, "We may not appreciate our freedom today because we have never suffered under tyranny." I stopped and wrote his thought down. Bailey knows suffering firsthand as his dad, my son-in-law, died prematurely just last year. Also, Bailey was born on the anniversary of that evil day of September 11th, the day America was attacked. So from his earliest years, he has experienced suffering and awareness of the evils of tyranny. Perhaps more than most of us, he knows that blessings cannot be taken for granted. On that recent July 4th, my family gathered to appreciate a great America and our exceptional freedom.

America is a great and an exceptional country. America is exceptional because of the ambitious goal of *"liberty and justice for all"* from tyrannical authority and whimsical legal processes. Exceptionalism is not a concept that Americans can boast of as if we have earned this special description or lived up to its meaning.

Exceptionalism is birthed from the superlative, radical political concept put forth as "liberty and justice for all" for which so many have died in wars from 1776 to 2014. Freedom to speak without fear of government reprisal, freedom to worship as we please, and the freedom to pursue personal ambition are the raisons d'etre for America and for American exceptionalism. America is **NOT** exceptional because we as a nation have always been honorable or even always been on the side of honor. Our nation has abused freedom far too many times both past and present; certainly we have underappreciated this gift of liberty.

America is taking this lavish freedom for granted today. Most of us consider freedom a right that is forever promised to America regardless of personal participation or not. Instead freedom is a blessing that the vast majority of people on every continent have never known. As we celebrate our liberty, most throughout the world will live in fear of government and non-government associations taking their freedom and possibly their lives away without trial, defense, or protestation. Fear of the powerful is the direct contraposition of liberty for all.

Freedom is not a birthright for anyone including Americans. Freedom is a blessing, I believe a blessing from our Creator. Freedom for most Americans is an unearned blessing; we have been given freedom by patriotic giants who have gone before. However, Americans today have the responsibility to value liberty as the rarest of all human environments in which to live, to protect it with every ounce of personal ability and collective unity, and to prove worthy ambassadors of freedom. Citizens of the United States may serve in government, as military or civilian, or not, but all Americans are called to serve the freedom of our nation.

How do we as citizens maintain our freedom? First, we learn from history the immeasurable sacrifice and the indelible dream that our fore-fathers have passed on to America today in the liberty we enjoy. Second, we learn from human nature that freedom is a springboard of life that ignites creativity, productivity, and happiness for all people. Third, we learn from current events that men, women, and children suffer immensely every day in the absence of freedom. We must consider ourselves blessed by God with liberty and commissioned by God to maintain liberty. Now, we must resolve to live our lives with thanksgiving and responsibility to ourselves, to God, and to others past, present, and future. We must live and encourage others to overcome with the enduring values of *GREATNESS, W—O—W—A.*

<u>Now is the perfect time to make the commitment.</u>

Therefore, we believe that freedom is an earned right. <u>This right can be lost if not honored and upheld.</u> The responsibility is mine.

So help me, God. <u>(My signature goes here.)</u>

Chapter 10

Work As Practiced By Max And Foxworth

*Our government must never promise to do for us what we must do for ourselves. And, we must never ask our government to give to us what we must earn through **work**.*

The American Kennel Club classifies the dogs of the world into seven sub-groups, Herding, Hound, Non-Sporting, Sporting, Terrier, Toy, and Working. These classifications are defined in part by the job that the dogs perform. Working, Herding, Hound, and Sporting classifications were dogs utilized in outside work assisting their masters. Terriers and Toys do their work in homes as family companions and in barns chasing out vermin.

When given the opportunity to choose a dog, I will always pick a canine friend from the Working Group. In New Orleans, I chose Max, a Rottweiler, to protect our family home after we were burglarized in the inner city. And later I chose Foxworth, a Newfoundland, to walk with me through the snowy woods of central Colorado. Both did their jobs with devotion and skill. They continually earned my love and respect by performing their instinctive work.

Work is an honorable virtue. Work is useful, creative, resourceful, purposeful, and encouraging. I never wonder what to do with myself. I can find work to do. I can create, assist, repair, clean, organize, or design. Monday morning begins on Sunday night when I prepare myself for work the next day. Max and Foxworth were always eager to be on the job; they never wanted a break.

Max kept our uptown property safe; we were never burglarized again after he came to work for us. On one occasion, a driver of a large passenger van mistook our yard for the street and jumped the curb, leveling our iron fence and shrubbery and stopping well into our back yard. When my wife called to alert me, I expected her to end the story by recounting an ugly encounter between Max and the stunned driver. To my delight, Max and the driver had made friends; he had adjusted to the sudden intrusion, and was sitting peaceably in the backyard. Max did his job everyday with wise discretion and honor.

My friend, Foxworth, was a dog bred to pull fishing nets to and from the boats in the very cold, fishing region of Newfoundland. True to his breed, Foxworth liked to pull on his large 20 ft. leash. He grabbed the free end of the rope in his teeth and with the other attached to his collar, we enjoyed our walk and each other's company.

I encourage Americans to find work. Even exhausting, difficult, and frustrating work can enrich our lives miraculously. Most of us work for our income to pay our living expenses. Some work in the home, some in factories, offices, schools, fields, shops, or highways. Even in these times of high unemployment, work and the preparation to work stimulates creativity, increases physical and mental activity, and cheers the heart. Unless physically, emotionally, or mentally hindered, Americans should all be workers.

As with Max and Foxworth, humans are designed to work. Work begets work. Energy utilized fends off boredom, depression, and the ill effects of laziness. In finding work to do, we discipline, develop, and define ourselves. We need not worry about how much we are paid; we will move up and increase our incomes in due time. As we develop skills, the world comes looking for us. As great Americans, we earn our wages with the skills we have learned and developed. We do not expect handouts from friends, family, churches, or the government. During unusual times, we may all need financial help; we can then exercise the grace to accept humbly the help and thereby be a blessing to the giver. However primarily, we should work in order to provide for ourselves and our families. Work in and around our families and our homes may not be paid in wages, but these responsibilities offer the rewards of fruitful work.

As the old adage goes, the absence of work or idleness is the devil's work shop; idleness can be very destructive. So let's get busy either preparing for our working careers or get busy doing our selected work. Let's earn our own living. Life can be unfair; employers can be unjust. But work is rewarding, uplifting, and life preserving. We should turn off the dream that someday our ship will come in, our lottery numbers will come up, or our long lost check will come in the mail.

What are we to do? **Learn a skill** for which others are willing to pay you as a competent worker. Even if others are better at that skill and the effort seems discouraging at times, we perform our work with diligence. We must find work, begin at the bottom, and be dependable and ambitious in doing a good job. Work, the willingness to work, and the skills of work will benefit us immensely.

If we find ourselves in a position to employ others, we should step up and employ willing and able workers, provide them the needed training and encouragement, and reward them fairly and generously. All of us started somehow, somewhere in our careers. We needed encouragement, guidance, and the opportunity to demonstrate our aptitudes. In our day, employing a worker is one way to support America and to prove the *GREATNESS* of one's own heart. Employers play a major role in serving America. Employers must willingly and generously compensate workers a fair and livable return in proportion to the monies earned through their labors.

The government must never be tempted to overreach and provide the money needed to support the individual. The role of providing income must remain with business and the entrepreneur. Throughout American history, the American people have permitted local governments to provide for public education up to and including skills training.

Today, the skills needed in the workplace are highly technical and sophisticated; willing workers need the required training. Local governments can cooperate with business leaders to offer skills training both in high school and post high school training as well as on the job training.

However, the responsibility to learn the skills necessary to be gainfully and productively employed in our society remains with the worker. Ultimately, government is not helping the national economy or the individual by financially supporting those who should be working and choose not to work.

Chapter *11*

Others Were Lili's Life.

*Our nation was commissioned by God to protect and enable the rights of everyone in a concerned and compassionate community. Our personal worth is found in serving **others**.*

Lili, our small beagle, was at her best when surrounded by others—dogs, children, puppies, whomever. Our family lived on a small, circle street with only eight homes and where neighbors knew each other well. One Saturday afternoon, a neighbor lady came to the door with Lili and a photo of our little beagle. She had joined a child's birthday party. The picture was of Lili with a party hat on her head and the most engaging expression on her face. Lili had joined the festivities of a child's birthday party and added to everyone's fun.

That incident was typical of our Lili. She loved others, and because she offered her love, she was loved by others in return. The only times I remember Lili getting into trouble was when she was penned up in the back yard by herself. Then she dug holes in the grass, in the flower bed, or around the fence. We couldn't stop her; she was lonely. How did we remedy her loneliness? We brought home Andi, a female golden retriever puppy as her new sister and companion.

Like other New Orleanians, in the fall of 1993, we had evacuated during Hurricane Andrew to Jackson, MS. The Mississippi state government was gracious enough to open the state park system as free temporary lodging for evacuees. Our entourage included two vehicles, four kids, my wife and I, all kinds of camping gear and, of course Lili. We had stopped for lunch when we spied a for sale sign for retriever puppies. We purchased Andi and she quickly became the perfect companion and mentor for Lili and for all of us. Andi was a lesson to us that in giving to others, we multiply the joy and love in our own lives.

As citizens of America, we cannot waste our lives in self-protection, self-promotion, or self-entertainment. We can become other focused. We can volunteer, visit, assist, support, serve, teach, protect, give, and love others. We can think about others from the defenseless infant to the oldest saint. We can get involved in neighborhoods, schools, churches, clubs, and with friends. Informal, occasional, pre-planned, spontaneous, or organized efforts, all offer the opportunities to be focused on others.

We can throw a party for someone; have someone over for dinner, take time to chat and to listen, or offer to help with a project—we can be other centered. I suggest that much of our misjudgment today stems from our self-centered focus. For example, a driver has car trouble which backs up traffic for miles. Other drivers become angry and speed off around the stranded driver. Perhaps we can stop to help. We are so impatient when another person interrupts our time and schedule; perhaps we can see another in need as an opportunity to serve. The gift of helping another person has the encouraging effect of lifting both the giver and the recipient. In doing so, we can recognize the significance of each other.

After Lili passed, we added Max to the family. Andi was left as our primary pet, but when Max came that role changed. Her response was totally selfless; she was willing to accept change. Max was a one year old Rottweiler and full of himself. Andi had to change her attitude from helping a rather slow moving Lili to being the wrestling partner for the new brute called Max. She adapted to Max and the two of them loved each other's company for many years. Andi and Max produced one litter of lovely puppies. We watched this transition and admired Andi's flexibility and willingness to serve, to be what others needed her to be. My wife has always said, "When I grow up, I want to be just like Andi."

We are not born being other centered. In fact, we begin life being necessarily self-focused. We naturally outgrow this infantile state into maturity. We are fulfilled when during our most active life, 6- 76 years, we serve and protect others. God gives to all of us talents and abilities enabling us to serve. Our talents are the gifts we give to another. Often the opportunities to serve come at some personal cost. Jesus once said that the grain must first die and be buried before it can produce the fruit for which the seed was created. The American way is to show compassion, protect the innocent, support the less fortunate, teach the young, and give of our resources.

These actions are so much more honorable and noble than Get, Take, Consume, Hide, and Indulge.

We have the simple joy of recognizing the significance of others: greet others enthusiastically, remember each other's names, let another go ahead, offer to help one another, and the list goes on. A quick gesture can brighten a whole day for another person. Noble morality and the steps to train ourselves in morality are better than and endure longer than any physical exercise or even spiritual discipline. Why? Because we are walking in the light of the best men and women who ever lived on any continent or at any time in history.

Chapter 12

Crystal Was My Wealthiest Dog.

*Our relationships and our personal character traits are the measures of real and lasting **wealth**. Family is our greatest asset and our most important gift to the future.*

Crystal was a wealthy dog. She was beautiful; she was picture perfect from her infancy until her passing. I adopted her from a local pet store when she was 7 weeks old. I was alone, starting a new life as a single-again man after fifteen years of marriage and without a family life which had included three kids. I had just graduated from Tulane University with a MBA, moved to the Westbank of the Mississippi River in New Orleans, and I was broke. I paid twenty-five dollars for Crystal; she helped to rebuild my life.

She had the typical tri-color markings of the Shetland sheep dog or sheltie. She grew to be about 45 lbs. and 28 inches high, so she was large for her breed. Yet she was perfect with an abundant, generous heart. She had a Mona Lisa smile; her personality was vivacious, playful, and winsome. She gave me hope because if she could love me perhaps, I could begin my life again. She gave to me from her abundant heart and generous spirit.

Crystal, of course, never owned a possession in her life, but she was wealthy beyond gold or silver. Her good heart remolded me into a family man. She never received a pay check, yet she gave to me every day of our life together. Before long, God granted me a wife and two more children. Before my divorce, I had lived with my three children, two girls and boy, and then He added one more girl and another boy. So I became wealthy again, and I have never been poor since. Crystal was the spark that ignited my heart with hope and love which opened my life to a new family.

The greatest achievement a man or woman will ever produce is a family. Two parents, kids, a dog, a cat, a mortgage, a car note (or two) are true wealth. I may never be financially wealthy, but my family loves me and that fills my heart with abundance. My family knows as did Crystal that I am not even close to perfect in any category of life. In fact, I may even be disappointing in some areas. But I have a family and I am part of a family; therefore I am a wealthy man.

Don't have a family? Start one. Try this. Get a dog. Or, better yet, call Compassion International (Compassion. com or 800-336-7676), for example, and sponsor or emotionally adopt a child. Learn to love, pick up after, care for when sick, discipline when necessary, pay the bills, defend against all attackers, and above all else walk your family through life. Talk to your newly formed family and listen to the spoken and unspoken clues of hunger, loneliness, and joy. Learn to share your life with someone else. We can learn to be family people. Learning to live with and serve another person through family makes us all better people.

Lili, our beagle, had puppies twice. She became a parent. WOW! Motherhood! Fatherhood! These are the two titles of nobility. Being a family man or woman, creating children and a home to nurture those children, and sending out young, responsible adults into society—these are the achievements that make us **GREAT**.

If God were to bless you with a lifelong, enduring love and give you offspring, then you are rich. If God's plan for you does not include marriage and/or children, then be assured you can still serve and assist others in their families and in our nation through multifaceted service occupations and avocations. Your immense importance will not be diminished.

I learned that past failures do not destroy this dream of family wealth. Our God can create a new, best plan, maybe not the one I thought I would have. But God can make us wealthy in family relationships and noble virtues. We must value family above all material possessions or man-made achievements.

Each family is different in many ways—how the roles play out, how the bills get paid, who does what and when, etc. Family is like a big marshmallow with multiple shapes, sizes, and colors. Family honors individual significance even as it teaches cooperation and compassion with others. But within this gooey, complicated grouping called family, life can flourish, reproduce, and give the next generation a strong foundation.

Family is the diamond of all relationships. ***Family is the moral womb for society.*** Over-estimating the importance of family is absolutely impossible. The loss of all moral values begins with the loss of family commitments in marriage and in sexuality. We cannot re-define family without suffering consequences.

Should we cast away the work of our forefathers and embark on a new and different set of principles? If we change or redefine the core values of America and of Americans, will we continue to be a **GREAT** nation?

Chapter *13*

Following Max's Example.

*Our peaceful society depends on the adherence by all to the laws of the land. If the law is to be changed, it is through public debate and submission to divine **authority**.*

Max followed commands, not the commands of Sit, Lie Down, Roll Over, but Come and Walk and Quiet. He was not interested in tricks for my amusement; he was not about to lose his individuality, independence, or personal power. Yet he knew I was the alpha dog in our relationship, and he understood that obedience and submission were not weaknesses but signs of character. He understood that I would never do him harm or use my position to humiliate or diminish him.

Together, we walked through the urban streets and gorgeous parks of Uptown New Orleans. This journey could be dangerous with rushing automobile traffic, buses roaring by, and discarded garbage along the curbs.

Obedience was a life preserver for Max and he needed it every day. At first, Max fought against the leash, thinking this device was sure to limit his fun. But after patient instruction and a firm hand, he learned that walking with me was better than taking control himself. Early in the training process, one afternoon walk, he pulled away from me and ran headlong with all his force into the door of a pickup truck. Fortunately, he was not hurt and the truck was not dented but wow! He was a different dog after that experience. He fell to the ground and as I rushed up to him, he shook his head as if to say, "Dad, I get it now. I shouldn't pull away from your leadership."

Sometimes I wonder if we understand the role that authority should take in our lives. Authority is provided by God and serves as a visible restraint to protect us and keep us from foolishness and mistakes. We are given first parents, then teachers, coaches, and pastors, then the legal system as authorities to reinforce good behavior. Proper, responsible, and sober behavior will never faint before the fearful consequences from authority. Only bad behavior will be punished and corrected, and that correction is the job of all authorities.

Understanding authority is the key to faith. I recall the Roman guard who asked Jesus to heal his child which Jesus promptly did. When Jesus offered to go to the guard's house, the guard said that a personal visit would not be necessary. Why? He understood authority; the Roman guard believed that Jesus had the authority from God and that a mere command from Jesus would heal his son. The guard's appreciation of authority and his faith in Jesus's authority moved the Son of God to perform the healing miracle. Furthermore, he received one of only three commendations for faith that Jesus ever gave to a person during His earthly ministry.

No human life will reach its fullest potential until obedience and submission to authority are practiced in every sphere of life. Television sports announcers comment that a rule violation at times is acceptable and possibly strategic unless it is caught by the officials and penalized. Even then, the violation might be better than letting the play go unhindered. Doesn't that make us cheaters?

Is winning the game so important that players and fans would lower our character to those of cheats? Is success more important than the way we play the game? I think not. Is it acceptable for me to cheat another as long as I don't get caught? Absolutely not! Doesn't cheating in any arena open the door to cheating in other aspects of life? Yes. How can we expect children to play by the rules if the adults do not? How can we be expected to be faithful in marriage if we cheat in business? Just as submission to the rules and obedience to authority are learned values for Max, so is this value necessary for all responsible citizens.

On occasion, laws have to be challenged through peaceful demonstrations, court room arguments, the voting booth, and public and private persuasions. The authorities have the right to expect that law abiding citizens will comply both with the spirit and law of the matter. The responsibility placed on all levels of authority is to be unbiased and reasonable. Rules by parents and teachers, laws established by governing bodies, or interpretations of laws by the courts must not favor some at the expense of others. Enforcement must be blind to race, gender, religion, age, or class. We are all called to obey the higher laws of God. We will all give an account for our actions and words. I know that I have broken in thought or action all of God's commands, and I am forever grateful to Jesus for forgiveness. But forgiveness does not lessen my responsibility to obey. His grace calls me to surrender my actions, appetites, thoughts, and ambitions to His highest purposes and authority.

Chapter 14

Andi Was And Is My Hero.

I introduced Andi earlier. She joined our family in 1993 and was a constant blessing until her passing during our evacuation from yet another hurricane in 2005. That makes Andi our hurricane dog. She joined us during Andrew and left us during Katrina. She lived with Lili and Max. She was the big sister to Lili and the wife to Max. This characterization may be humanizing her excessively, but Andi's behavior proved her worth.

Andi's work was to be the companion dog to the other dogs. She helped to improve Lili's youthful waywardness. She guided Max into understanding his responsibility to stay in the fenced yard and protect our property. Andi never complained when the other dog was getting attention because she understood her role as the support or helper dog. She was never noisy even if the other was barking at various distractions.

Andi never fought over the food bowl or got angry when the other dog ate the remaining kibbles in her bowl. Andi faithfully nursed her pups and while eager to see them off to good homes, she was never impatient with their demands. She was a giver, a sharer, a self-sacrificing example of all the exemplary traits of a golden retriever. She was a GREAT DOG. She was other centered at the core of her being. While I mowed the lawn, she jumped into the back of the Jeep and through the open tailgate, she watched my every move. She was helping me.

I describe her as completely non-possessive, unselfish and yet passionately involved with every level of our family. Each of us felt we were her favorite. She was enthusiastic about our family. She belonged and she never wandered off. For Andi, our family relationships were her wealth. She could be walked off leash along the Intercoastal Canal near Belle Chasse, LA; she could be completely trusted to come when called. She made us a richer family through her presence and love.

As a puppy, she must have required correction, but I can't remember a single behavioral issue. Once when Lili, our beagle, delivered puppies, it was Andi who gathered them and brought them to their mama for their first nursing. Lili constantly neglected her young, not because she didn't care; she was just always socializing. In contrast, Andi never tried our patience; she was obedient with a glance. For those of us who know dogs, we know that these special canine friends understand more than some might think. Andi was submissive to Max and yet did not allow him to get too rough and mistreat her because he was bigger and stronger than she.

Andi taught me the virtues of **_W—O—W—A_**. In the next chapter, I will repeat the call to all of us to reclaim the virtues of ***Work, Others, Wealth, and Authority***. Our nation must regain the traits that made America great. Frequent scandals, sexual misbehaviors, family breakups, financial scams, and senseless, planned and random killings signal that our national culture is critically ill? **Shouldn't we take action to change these calamities?**

We have replaced the virtue of work with the pursuits of leisure and pleasure. We have replaced service to others with insistence on self-attention. Materialism and the pursuit of more and bigger possessions have replaced the virtue of building better families and communities. And without question, we are more distrustful and rebellious toward all authority than is beneficial for us. America can be and can do better. We must overcome the cancer of self-gratification or narcissism.

We must return to the proper respect of ***Work, Others, Wealth*, and *Authority***. We must honor the workers, the servants, the parents and teachers, and the authorities. Americans can make radical changes. Replacing the values that do not build ***GREATNESS*** with the proven values that created our nation will be the essential place to start. Andi is my example; we certainly didn't teach her the values by which she lived. These values came from her Creator. We too can be led by God to the better, higher values of our natures.

In America, our governments are accumulating enormous debt with the vain hope that the bill for this debt is never delivered. We are developing a wealthy class that is living in luxury beyond belief while the middle and lower classes are struggling sometimes losing hope.

Our families, neighborhoods, and schools are divided and failing to inspire noble character, leaving children without role models and adult friends. We are legalizing behavior that will not produce educated, responsible, and mature adults. From the violence of street gangs and school shootings to the commercial frauds of business and the scandals in government, we are destroying our nation, our faith in each other, and our cooperation with each other. We are falling away from **GREATNESS**.

In conclusion, heroic, noble character based on strong values is diminishing within our nation. In growing pockets of America, anarchy is impacting our country. Confusion and misdirection are rampant throughout America. Much of our workforce is not educated or motivated. America creates too many single parent families locked in poverty. America's economy at one time was built by agricultural and industrial craftsmen and entrepreneurs. Now we have become money changers under the mysterious titles of hedge fund managers and merger arbitrage specialists. The explosion of crime and violence on our streets is resulting in an even greater explosion of weapons in America. These are only a few examples of the anarchy burying America and its values.

We have exchanged
the work ethic for the idol of pleasure,
the joy of service for negligent apathy,
the family for materialism,
and abiding the law for lawlessness.

I am not the first nor am I am alone in observing that America's present path will not realize the peace, prosperity, or happiness we desire. History proves that lowered values weaken individuals and in turn weaken society at large. A valueless nation cannot build a consensus to govern and therefore, cannot resolve strategic issues in that society.

Instead of solving problems, our federal government is passing the issues on for another time and place that will never come. The Biblical indictment is that "every man is doing what was right in his own eyes." The Bible records that a weakened society is easily overtaken or splintered by a dominating leader or movement as recorded in the Old Testament book of Judges. ***Everyone doing what is right in his own eyes will be the direct cause for the destruction of America***. The American way of exercising our freedoms while being guided by noble values has been lost ***under the idolatry of pleasure, self, materialism, and rebellion***. We can and we must overturn the path we are now following. But how?

Chapter 15

W—O—W—A Say It Again
W—O—W—A

The American system of government is not broken; however, we, the people operating the system require a major overhaul of our moral values. We must adopt the following:

Statement of Shared Values

We thank you, God, for the endless blessings of freedom and we joyfully assume responsibility for maintaining our freedom.

We hereby affirm these statements of shared responsibilities.

*Our government must never promise to do for us what we must do for ourselves. And, we must never ask our government to give to us what we must earn through **work**.*

*Our nation was commissioned by God to protect and enable the rights of everyone in a concerned and compassionate community. Our personal value is found in serving **<u>others</u>**.*

*Our relationships and our personal character traits are the measures of real and lasting **<u>wealth</u>**. Family is our greatest asset and our most important gift to the future.*

*Our peaceful society depends on the adherence by all to the laws of the land. If the law is to be changed, it is through public debate and submission to divine **<u>authority</u>**.*

Therefore, we believe that freedom is an earned right. <u>This right can be lost if not honored and upheld.</u> The responsibility is mine.

So help us, God.

*What conclusions can we draw from the confusion we see around us? Will we complain or will we change? More noble personal and national values will save us as individuals and as a nation. Today, our culture and therefore, our nation is weakening from the inside out. We can and we must decide now to change our values. **The essence of America is not conservatism, liberalism, or libertarianism; the essence of our democracy is moral.***

The morality of our nation will determine our future success. Will you join me and many others in signing and agreeing to the values of the Statement of Shared Values?

What is my vision for America?

1. *A nation at WORK stimulates creativity. Creativity means a growing economy.*
2. *A nation for OTHERS teaches civility. Civility builds a peaceful community.*
3. *A nation of WEALTH produces generosity. Generosity takes care of the less fortunate.*
4. *A nation under AUTHORITY yields unity. Unity solves the problems of the day.*

WORK stimulates creativity because as in the old English proverb reminds us "necessity is the mother of invention." Creativity invents practical solutions; solutions start businesses and businesses employ people. People buy goods and services which increases demand and demand increases creativity. Creativity then repeats itself. Our innate ambitions and skills generate an economy founded upon personal gain and the good of others.

And so forth, civility enables a peaceful and safe environment for every individual in cooperation with others. Wealth is built and then shared with the community **NOT** through government taxes but through the *GREATNESS* of the human heart. Authority safeguards the unity of the whole and the rights of the individual within the social process.

Chapter 16

Let's Be Great Again

If we can agree that liberty leads to
creativity and prosperity
and that a united community offers the
best protection for our liberty,
then a properly functioning community will provide
the highest levels of freedom and therefore,
cultivate increased individual productivity and
Personal Happiness.
For a community to function at a mature,
problem-solving, freedom-
producing level, the majority of
citizens must embrace and
demonstrate shared, noble values.
To do otherwise leads to the
Anarchy of Self-indulgence.

These shared values must be the individual
and the collective character
virtues taught in families, schools,
and places of worship,
then, practiced
daily in our businesses, in government,
and in our personal lives.
America's proven and successful
formula was designed with the
Key Ingredients of Shared Values:

Work: self-support,
Others: self-denial,
Wealth: self-worth, and
Authority: self-governing.

Therefore, we can conclude that shared values or the lack thereof will determine the success or failure of America. America can provide the greatest freedoms only when the citizenry is responsible to uphold our shared values. For the United States to remain great and free, we must passionately pursue these shared values. **Americans individually have the dominant role in determining the future of our nation.** We can take the reins of America to stop our moral train wreck and head directly to *GREATNESS*. Let us be **GREAT** again.

In the absence and ignorance of personal values, government with a disingenuous sense of compassion will step forward to grant financial favors and to control behaviors consistent with the state's intrusion. Four resultant actions have emerged in America in the following steps:

1) Excessive personal dependence on government programs,
2) Excessive government agencies to regulate the programs,
3) Excessive taxation to pay for the programs, and
4) Ultimately, more government control and fewer individual freedoms.

Is this a formula for a nation destined to **GREATNESS**? **Absolutely not!!** This is a formula for failure on the personal and national levels.

With the increase of federal control, four reactions among the people will emerge:

1) Some elitists will lobby government policies for their own purposes and will hijack the government to favor themselves.
2) Other individuals and businesses will gorge themselves on the public treasury to take whatever is available for the taking.
3) Organized groups will emerge that see big government as hostile to their rights and will foment fear and aggression against the government. Our nation will be in gridlock except for the occasional new questionable, government program.

Lastly and most devastating, 4) **most Americans will be passive.** They will feel powerless to change such Un-American control and will retreat from the issues and from the elections. Personal ambition, utilitarian creativity, and social participation is stifled when the government over-promises and over-reaches. For example, too few of us even care to be informed and to vote. Doing nothing will allow the lowest influences in a culture to dominate. We must educate ourselves about our Constitution and about the American way. Then, we must participate in the process to restore America.

In any or all of the above four cases, the American way of life will suffer under a government that is distrusted, disunified, and dysfunctional. This turmoil cannot last indefinitely; unsolved issues are mounting. We note the rise in national debt, the explosion of illegal immigration, the gridlock in Congress, and the incredible deceit from our government just to name a few unsolved problems. Do these conditions make us feel more empowered and more protected by our government? I think not. We as Americans must take action to regain the personal values and the role of limited government that will reclaim our **GREATNESS.** Government overreaches its limited role when personal values decrease. In the absence of individual virtue, government is tempted to fill the void with its own pretentious policies and programs that will consistently disappoint and fail.

We can and we must take back our country from the destructive elements of lowered personal values and increased government control. We, the people, can re-establish the America way. **How? Very simply stated: 1) we as citizens return to higher moral values and 2) we elect and demand higher moral decision making by our leaders.** The battles and transitions of the Civil Rights Movement during the 1960's exemplify America lifting itself from the immorality of segregation to the morality of integration. However imperfect and painful the process and though we are still witnessing racial prejudice, we are marching to a better, higher ground than that on which we once stood.

The magic for America is that free and moral men and women produce devoted families, prosperous businesses, and peaceful communities. Politicians must go when they do not uphold the magic. Under the influence of moral-less men and women, America will be perverted with unscrupulous yet powerful elite, broken families, greedy businessmen, corrupt politicians, and immoral lifestyles.

Chapter *17*

An American Destiny

We study and celebrate the enduring and successful American spirit. America has shown a great spirit at critical times in its history, and certainly our American values have enabled a powerful "can-do" spirit among our population. Our spiritual values can and do produce greatness. Again, **GREATNESS** does not mean the greatest any more than Max should be considered the greatest among all my other dogs, Foxworth, Max, Andi, Crystal, or Bo. However, our American values have led us at pivotal times to accomplish great achievements and to experience God's favor in peace and prosperity. America was founded with the definable and worthwhile ideals of life, liberty, and the pursuit of happiness.

The American political ideals have been described as the pursuits of free enterprise, individual freedom, limited government, and a strong national defense. However, we must dig deeper into the foundations of these political goals. What values at the individual level have caused this country to demonstrate ***GREATNESS*** in creativity, in generosity, in productivity, and in unity? And, will these underlying values lead us again to solve our problems, guide decision-making, and reclaim ***GREATNESS***?

I submit that the personal values of an ambitious work ethic, an other-centered generosity, a non-materialistic definition of wealth, and deep respect for authority have created the fertile soil for American ***GREATNESS***. These values are deeply held Christian beliefs. Furthermore, faith in God and in His Bible is the bedrock of America even if not all of our forefathers were Christians. America is largely ignorant of our historical, Judeo-Christian values and is mistakenly turning from these foundational values. The result is our current moral confusion.

An important step in solving our moral confusion is a radically new type of leader. We need a leader who understands and demonstrates personally America's formula for **GREATNESS**. We need a leader who is willing and able to point us to the benefits and necessity of higher values and principled living. America is calling for fresh and profoundly different type of leader. We are looking for a leader that discovers solutions rooted in morality and rejects the partisan blindness of re-election and power. As Americans, we know that we are on the wrong moral path. We need a leader who will call us to the higher, nobler paths of morality. Many are praying for this desperate need.

The application of these principles demands vigorous debate, we should expect good men and women to differ on any relevant issue. The issues we face in America today are so incendiary and divisive that new policy decisions alone will not suffice. ***This hour in America demands courageous, moral, and political leadership.*** The leader must win the argument by his/her character and wisdom not through deceptive, empty words. Manipulating the election and the legislative process to gain the upper hand is not leadership. Political favoritism or providing favors in exchange for votes and/or money is not leadership. The motives for leadership must not be party affiliation, power, or even re-election but the welfare of the people. Leaders do not serve themselves; leaders serve the people. Public officials especially lawyers, judges, and elected officials, those entrusted to maintain justice and order, are servants of God and ultimately responsible to Him (NT Romans 13).

Serving in government is at the consent of the governed, not through beguiling the public with simplistic, manipulative television advertising. We are bombarded with 30 second ad campaigns which incriminate an opponent with little regard for balanced discussions on the issues. Money and its influence must be removed from the election and the legislative processes. I suggest we discourage all 30-60 second political commercials and replace them with longer, public service discussions between the candidates. This simple change, while upsetting the television and radio networks, would sharply reduce the money needed to finance a political campaign. If we can reduce the money needed to run for office, then the influence of money in politics could be diminished. Changes in the policies and processes will only occur when we make changes in the way we evaluate our leaders. Americans must seek men and women committed to unselfish values.

The voting public must be involved, informed, and willing to support the candidate and his/her values, not manipulated by clever words that deceive rather than inform. These changes in values and in processes are revolutionary and demand an essential paradigm shift. Policy changes will occur after we, the American citizens, first find agreement on the values we choose for America.

Before we can decide issues and solve problems, we must discuss and find agreement in our values as Americans. Let us remove from national and local public office those whose character does not match the values we choose for America.

Holding up a mirror to our nation and taking a candid look at the society we have become will both shock us and call us to change. Do we as Americans desire or revere the nation we now inhabit? If not, then we can demand the changes to uphold virtue above political party or personal gain. Let's ask ourselves the following:

Do we expect people of able body and mind to work for their living?
Do we respect others regardless of race, religion, gender, or age?
Do we believe that the best measure of an individual is his/her character and not his/her material wealth?
Do we accept the authority of law and of law enforcement at every level?

The answer is *YES, we do*. Please join me and many others in praying that God will raise up values-driven leaders. I pray that God changes me and my fellow

Americans into values-directed people. The opportunity to change has not escaped. We can support more noble leaders and turn our nation toward **GREATNESS**.

America is ripe for a public debate on values not just a debate on policies, political parties, or personalities. What candidate(s) best illustrate the values and principles of **GREATNESS**? We can and should make wholesale changes in America's leadership; however, the revolution in values must begin with you and me. In the next chapter, we will discuss how to make this change. We will know that this new adventure has started when we remove from political leadership those individuals who have enriched themselves while in office and install new leaders who demonstrate the values that we, the people, hold dear.

In our American democracy, the people should not be victims of an inefficient, self-aggrandizing government. **We can change the way Washington works by first changing our values and then replacing our elected leaders.**

The functions of national government are threefold which are:

1) Protect the people from physical attacks both internally and around the globe,
2) Protect the people from those who would financially cheat others, and
3) Protect the public use of land, air, and water which must be shared by all. Beyond these three, the federal government is overstepping its role and definition.

Chapter 18

Significance Lives On And On

This chapter is the most difficult to write. My canine friends have now passed away. Crystal is dead. Lili is also. Max and Andi are dead. Yet they live on in my memories of the heart and of the mind because they lived **great, significant** lives, and my family and I loved them. They will never be really gone because they taught me how to love and how to live in ways that transcend selfishness and self-conceit.

In just the past two weeks, my family has also suffered the loss of three more of our beloved pets, Foxworth, Bo, and Pearl, our wonderful and devoted cat. The lesson we are learning is that life can be unexpectedly fragile; we have no guarantees regarding how long our lives or legacies will continue. Our freedoms will be lost unless we choose the values that will last.

The Bible says that "righteousness exalts a nation." I have learned a corollary that ***righteousness exalts the individual too***. Living rightly adds meaning, character, and nobility to a life that transcends size, intellect, talent, success, and even time. Living rightly adds blessedness, honor, and dignity to our ordinary days. Blessedness is God's gift to those who choose His way of life. Honor determines how we are remembered by others. Dignity is the respect we have for ourselves. **Blessedness, Honor and Dignity follows the life worth living or the life lived well.**

Crystal, Lili, Max, Andi, Bo, and Foxworth lived with honor, and my family will always think of them with dignity. Their ***GREATNESS*** was as visible and unmistakable as sunlight in August in the Rio Grande valley.

Americans can live our lives with values and be remembered with honor. Or, we can live for pleasure, self, materialism, and rebellion. I raised a mirror before our nation in the last chapter in the form of four questions. Now I ask the same questions expressed differently.

Should the objective of life be to maximize leisure and pleasure?

Should I live as if I am the only one that matters?

Should the one who dies with the most material possessions really win?

Should we resist the rules, standards, and laws of society and of God yet remain free?

The answer is *NO, we must not*. Popular culture encourages us to believe that time off and scoffing at work altogether are the happiest ways of life. In addition, our culture teaches that happiness is found by looking out for ourselves, by acquiring more shiny and new possessions, and by pulling the wool over the eyes of morality. The canine companions with whom I have walked and shared my life were not tempted by such deceptions. Our inspirational pets chose the high road that earned them dignity, honor, and the blessings of God.

GREATNESS will come to those who live as follows:

1) **Work hard,**
2) **Serve others,**
3) **Appreciate true non-material wealth, and**
4) **Respect all levels of authority.**

The self-respect and the respect from others gained through a life of noble values will overcome failure, disappointment, and personal limitations.

The Bible provides a perfect example of living by noble values. The widow gave two cents into the offering, a tiny sum of money, yet she is revered. Jesus said of her that she surrendered more true wealth than those who gave much more. She gave from her heart and with all of her heart. The widow is remembered with admiration through the Scripture forever. She is blessed because she lived with GREAT values.

I have known many great people, my dad, Preston Childers, a coach, Jimmy Juarez, Kathy Weckel, a friend, and Herschel Martindale, a pastor. Each one exemplifies one or more of the values that define GREATNESS.

My dad taught me by his example the virtue of **work**. Kathy thought of **others** first; she made me her friend by remembering my name. Herschel taught me the **wealth** of family by loving his own family. Coach Juarez shook my hand and taught me to respect **authority**. Remember the special people in your life; didn't each one exemplify one or more of the *W—O—W—A* values?

I will always remember these great people for their memorable contribution to my life. Honor is achieved by living with great values. **America was, is, and will be great to the degree that we exemplify and inspire great values.**

America will never, never solve our individual or national issues without changing our values, renewing what we value in life and in America. Change to virtuous living is difficult, but not impossible, so I humbly offer a plan of action. Plant four simple words in your mind and ask God to teach you how to live them. He will do the hard work of transforming us and creating *GREATNESS* in our characters. If you and I will ingest and apply these values along with millions of other Americans, God will grant us the mercy to change.

Right living exalts any nation or individual who adopts right values. Right values add beauty, dignity, happiness, and productivity to the lives that we live. This generation may be remembered as the one which chose right values, right living, and God's blessings.

"God bless America" does not happen by wishing it so in song or at the conclusions to our speeches; God blesses those who choose right living.

Changing our values is a work of God in our lives. The most enduring and penetrating motivation for right living is the redeeming love of God. Our responsibility today is to allow truth into our lives as precious seeds of thought.

The values of ***Work***, ***Others***, ***Wealth***, and ***Authority*** can be planted and nurtured in our minds and lives. God will produce the fruit of right living beginning in our hearts and then flowing out into our daily lives. O God, let this change begin in me.

Americans will have to turn away from the lifestyles with which we have grown up and to which we are now accustomed. For the sake of the next generation, parents must begin living and teaching right values, teachers must expect moral thinking from themselves and from their students, pastors must teach the biblical truths of sin, salvation, and God, and government must live within a balanced budget. We are in this fight for right living together.

Families, schools, and churches are more important to America's future than the White House, Congress, or the Courts. Parents, teachers, and pastors are the real super heroes in America. Proverbs says, "By wisdom houses are built." The wise way and the blessed way is God's way. The debate is: ***What values or principles will shape America today?***

Families and children thrive with devoted fathers and mothers. Business is profitable with win-win transactions. Politics are productive with wise, unselfish leaders. Schools teach effectively with educated and committed teachers. Morality makes all the difference between solving problems or kicking them down the road or even making the problems worse through neglect and/or foolishness.

Right living also ignites boldness, confidence, and courage. Proverbs 28:1 declares "The wicked flee when no one is pursuing, but the righteous are as bold as a lion." This boldness is akin to the golfer on the first tee who through practice and training <u>knows</u> that his tee shot will clear the bunker at the corner of the dogleg and be in position for a low score. So called "luck" is not a peculiar happenstance but the result of proper preparation and timely action. When with clear conscience and dedication to do the right, we act in accordance with morality and faith we can be decisively bold in our actions and our plans. Under the paralysis of guilt and fear, we tend to do nothing or at best act too late to accomplish meaningful benefits.

GREATNESS is a message of HOPE and not of despair. No breakthrough technology is required. No cure for a deadly virus is needed. A huge asteroid is not headed for America. The answer to our present crises can be implanted within the American soul. Let us smile at the future as we rebuild ourselves, our families, schools, places of worship, and of course, our government. Let's reignite moral character and courage within the United States of America.

"Blessed is the nation whose God is the Lord." Psalms 33:12

Chapter 19

Everyone Loves An Underdog.

Let there be no misunderstanding; the United States is in a battle for her character and her freedom. We have lost much of our previous prestige among the industrialized nations. We possess the world's strongest currency and yet we are deeply in debt. America supports the most developed educational system in the world and still illiteracy profligates while low high school graduation rates dominate large pockets of our country. We educate the best trained health care professionals in the world, and we cannot find a way to pay for medical care for millions of Americans. Therefore, illnesses go undetected and uncured because health care is locked behind economic doors. Our military and police are unmatched in their capabilities and dedication, but we cannot prevent irrational violence on home soil or anywhere in the world. Unemployment is rampant, not for want of jobs, but for want of trained, motivated men and women to fill those jobs.

The U.S. resources are tied up in the knots of special interests competing rather than cooperating in order to find solutions. Our complete denial of the worth of every person is making us fearful of and cold to each other rather than helpful to one another. We are so busy perverting right living that we blissfully ignore the fact that our nation is crumbling under abuse, violence, crime, scandal, fraud, and addiction. Our politicians cannot be trusted; our pastors are often irrelevant and unbiblical, and our businessmen are too often seeking excessive profit at the expense of their customers, communities, and employees.

I suggest that many of the shockingly horrific crimes, scandals, and evils in America can be explained by the moral contamination of our culture through our unhealthy, unwise, and stubborn rejections of decent morality.

America is now a toxic, diseased culture; we are destroying our youth, our families, our problem solving abilities, our productivity, and ultimately our freedom.

Enough!! When my beloved Foxworth was fighting for his life, the vet had not found the diagnosis or the cure. My wife and I were treating him and comforting him every way we could. Still our combined efforts did not cure him and soon he passed. We have felt a great sadness with our inability to save our Foxworth and other animal friends. However, the absence of a diagnosis or cure is not the case in America. We know the diagnosis. We have the cure. America has lost its way for two reasons: 1) **We have forgotten our American values** and 2) **our government is controlling too many aspects of our lives.**

I do not argue that we are a little, temporarily lost. America is desperately lost, confused, and uncertain about the future. We are calling the morally wrong right and defining the morally right as wrong. We, you and I, have lost the values that made America great. We want free time more than time learning a skill and working at that skill. We want to be first on the highways, in the stores, and in our relationships rather than serving and caring for others. We pursue more money and more pleasure, and we are willing to sacrifice promises, character, and our families in the pursuit of self-indulgence. We insist that no one tell us right from wrong at any level; we insist the authorities stop the other guy and leave us alone. We have made gods of the wrong values. We are practicing idolatry and permitting anarchy to invade our nation.

As if anarchy was not enough, our governmental malaise is a spectacle of inefficiencies, deceit, and overreach. The courts can't decide right from wrong; they don't know the right. The legislature cannot protect right living; they do not choose wise living for their own lives. The President cannot lead in the path of wise unselfishness; he is pursuing his own agenda. Personal financial gain has replaced the good for all sentiment that once dominated our policy decisions. Money and power have corrupted sound political action.

The cure for individuals and for America is a change in personal values. The spiritual awakenings of the 18th, 19th, and 20th centuries in America prove that a faith based revival is possible. By God's grace, this generation of Americans too can raise its values. To be guided by higher values rather than natural desires is a difficult but important change to make. The change will be more like a revolution of moral character.

I want to introduce someone who can make change and *GREATNESS* possible: His name is Jesus. The most powerful value of all is our personal relationship with God through faith in Jesus Christ. Being right with God makes all the other honorable values possible.

The revolution in our relationship with God begins with a simple, but sincere prayer, "Lord Jesus, I confess my selfishness; I confess my rebellion against You. Come into my life, forgive my sin and lead me in righteousness." Through this prayer, He forgave and changed me. I am nowhere near the man I should be but thank God, I am different than I might have been. **God's first work in our lives is to bring life renewing forgiveness. Forgiveness is the life transfusion that motivates all the moral changes that happen later.** We begin by acknowledging our fault before God and inviting Him to take charge. God's love and God's forgiveness will empower the change.

I am praying that politicians, businessmen, spiritual leaders, and each American accept the call of God to repent of selfishness and rebellion. Ask humbly for Jesus to bring peace with God and to lead to higher values and principles. I ask men, women, boys, and girls to say "Yes" to God's authority over our lives. We have the opportunity now to hear the drumbeat of destruction all around us and to begin our individual lives and America anew with the values that will make us right with God. We are the moral underdogs; Jesus is the hope and the cure.

Repentance from our past sins and *faith in Jesus* for forgiveness are the answers. This answers are near; the answers are from the heart. The Bible says, "Believe in the Lord Jesus, and you will be saved, you and your household" (Acts 16:31).

This belief is ***not part*** of the answer. This belief is the ***complete*** answer. Right now many of the issues we face as individuals and as a nation seem impossible to solve. However, God will lead us to find the solutions that are currently hidden from us. **Living in a right relationship to God, our Creator, is the path to the solutions for the problems that now seem impossible.** God is offering the personal and national solutions.

No one and no nation is beyond His touch. No one is insignificant, no one is too powerful, and nothing is insurmountable. No personal or public problem is beyond His remedy. We must submit to and trust in Jesus; He will give us a new birth, new lives, and new direction. I trust in Jesus as my Savior, and in Him I have hope. God's love was His motivation for our redemption; His Son, Jesus, is the solution for you, for me, and for America. A friend once said to me, "God loves me best." He further explained that God loves everyone best; His best love is His only level of love. We can receive His love, forgiveness, and life principles into our lives and into our nation. **America can be healed. God can and desires to give us a new birth individually and nationally.**

Chapter 20

W—O—W—A   Applied

In the movie, *Gladiator*, the hero, Maximus, asks this question: *"When is a slave greater than the Emperor?"*

The American Declaration of Independence provides this answer: *"That whenever any Form of Government becomes destructive of these ends, it is the Right of the People to alter or to abolish it, and to institute new Government, laying its foundation on such principles and organizing its powers in such form, as to them shall seem most likely to effect their Safety and Happiness."*

In other words, when the emperor is destructive to the pursuits of free men, then a new nation of former slaves should be formed from the principles and values that the former slaves know are right and just.

The American Revolution was fought in order to gain freedom from the then tyrannical British Empire.

Our great nation was formed by great leaders and a great population sacrificing its wealth and its temporary well-being for the lifestyle we now call the American way. If today America continues to lose it values and principles, **GREATNESS** will evaporate as the frost under the morning sun. Our freedoms will collapse along with our virtue.

GREATNESS is cultivated; no human, except for Jesus, is born with this characteristic. As children, we can have *GREATNESS* modeled before us through our parents, taught to us by our schools and churches, reinforced by authority, but ultimately nobility or **_GREATNESS_ of character is the sum of our choices**.

Our choices are the product of the character we are within and our desire to live noble lives.

Again, walking Foxworth suggests a lesson on moral behavior. One early morning, he smelled out a discarded Styrofoam box of rotting food. He lurched for it as if he were starving. He knew full well that a bowl of nutritious and tasty fresh kibbles was at the house. He had never missed a meal. "Then why, Foxworth? That old, stinky food would make you sick and never satisfy your hunger. You know that, and then why not wait until you get home?" He soon experienced the result of following his poor instincts; he was reminded that he shouldn't eat garbage. We have to make the same types of choices as individuals and as a nation.

An oft repeated statement is: America is great because of our Constitution. Our U.S. Constitution is supernaturally unique; it is unique because the document was written by unique people in search of unique freedoms and a demand for a unique government to safeguard those freedoms. No country had been founded before on freedom of religion, freedom of speech, freedom of property ownership, freedom of personal rights, and freedom from government intervention. We were then and we are now unique, divinely commissioned to experience freedom. The right to pursue the personal choices of life and happiness was recognized as a right granted by the Creator. This freedom did not emanate from men or from government and therefore, it should not be removed or restricted by man or government except by mutual consent for the good of all.

Our US Constitution reflects noble values; however, ***it will not nor can it create or rebuild our lost moral values***. Our choices must be controlled by a value system which promotes consistent living to our Constitution— living that respects ***Work***, ***Others***, ***Wealth***, and ***Authority***.

Americans are no longer consistently and intentionally upholding these values. America's freedom and its very existence are **incompatible** with the choices we are now making. Individual choices of right over wrong were essential to America's past and now, equally essential to America's future.

Selfishness, self-centeredness, self-gratification, and rebellion are incompatible values with a great America. As a result of mis-directed values, our personal decisions are immoral, our leaders are unethical, and our businessmen are greedy. Our legislatures are confused and our society is weakening. We no longer seek the morally right but we seek the pleasurable, the riches of money, and the rewards for self. Immoral living leads to illogical thinking and vice versa.

The wise King Solomon once wrote, "There is a way that seems right to a man, but the end thereof is the way of death." The right way is NOT written inside our hearts, but it is written by God and given to us in the Bible. Let us not look to our instincts, cravings, or even our needs to determine the right choice, but let us look to God.

Causes of and solutions to our national problems are available in the choices that we, the people, make. The solution to national debt is for all of us to expect less from the government and more from self-reliance. The solution to violence of all kinds is a more noble love and respect for others and their property. The solution to unemployment is the worker preparing himself or herself for a skilled profession in our high tech economy, business owners/ managers and stockholders accepting their responsibilities to employees, their families, and to their communities with a long term perspective on profits. The solution to immigration is living by the rule of law both by protecting our borders and by submitting to the laws governing the employment of undocumented workers. These concepts are not difficult. Implementation is only made difficult because from the top of society down, we embrace selfish and contradictory values; therefore, we are falling for unwise choices.

From the worker to the leader, Americans are choosing to live mis-valued lives. From the citizen to the President, we are choosing self-indulgent values. We need radical change. However, we cannot force character change on anyone. We must win the argument between a noble, principled nation and a nation of ignoble lust. The argument for right values can be logical and wise, persuading the mind and then convicting the heart of America.

Many of our national leaders create divisions among us and do not explore solutions for the nation as a whole. Our public debate is characterized by name-calling, criticizing, and not representing higher values. Both the political Right and the Left are guilty of seeking the prestige of power above service to our nation. Politicians use negative advertising, negative speech, and negative media to lambaste the other side without addressing values. We are now divided as a nation almost in half over national debt, abortion, immigration, gun control, drug legalization, gay rights, and many other major issues. Where do we go from here?

I suggest we vote out and refuse financial support to every social, economic, and political leader or organization from the White House to Nashville, from New York City to Los Angeles, and from Wall Street to Main Street—every form of influence that is not consistent with our American values. WE, the people, can make the difference to save America. I suggest our leaders on every level change their values to reflect more noble, wise, and honorable choices.

Also, we, the people, have the responsibility to walk humbly before God and to follow His ways. Part of that responsibility is to elect more noble leadership.

A perfect example of ***W—O—W—A*** applied and of God's reward for it surfaces in Ruth of the Old Testament book bearing her name. A young foreign woman is told to be practical. Her father-in-law and husband are dead; her sister-in-law has returned to her birth family. Ruth should go back too. Instead Ruth honors her vow to Naomi, her mother-in-law, goes to work as a pauper in the fields, and supports both herself and Naomi. When a wealthy landowner, Boaz, notices her values, he helps her garner food from his fields and ultimately marries her. Ruth is a woman driven by the values of self-support, kindness to others, valuing her new family vow before her native family's wealth, and obedience to the customs of her day.

The Bible records: *"But Boaz answered her, 'All that you have done for your mother-in-law since the death of your husband has been fully told to me, and how you left your father and mother and your native land and came to a people that you did not know before. The LORD repay you for what you have done, and a full reward be given you by the LORD, the God of Israel, under whose wings you have come to take refuge!'"* (Ruth 2:11, 12).

Our responsibility is to stand beside
her (America) and guide her.

"God Bless America"

God Bless America,
Land that I love.
Stand beside her, and guide her,
Through the night with the light from above.

God's blessings are not accidents nor are His blessings assumed inheritances from one generation to another. God blesses those who through His grace walk in accordance with His ways. Our generation has an obligation to the past and a responsibility to the future to apply the American way to America.

Chapter 21

Living Indoors

The freedom to live indoors near the people they love is gratifying for all dogs. Bo loved our homes, but he had to be trained. My wife and I often boasted that we could take Bo anywhere. He was perfectly housebroken, well mannered, and quiet. One beautiful, sunny Sunday afternoon, Bo, my wife, and I were motorcycling through southern Mississippi. We were looking for and found a church service to attend. However, the weather was too hot to leave Bo outside so we asked if we could bring him inside. After the local members looked Bo over, they invited all of us to attend their evening service. Bo was, of course, true to his form and behaved like the good dog that he was. Bo was housebroken in every way and could always be trusted to please us and delight others.

Similarly, in social settings, when living with others, human behavior must conform to the written and unwritten rules of community. Earlier, I referred to both the written documents of the US Constitution, etc. and the unwritten code of the American way. Our words and actions are governed by the law and by the common courtesies of our society. Learning to behave ourselves and not disturb the general well-being and comfort of others is part of maturity. At times, the public good should trump or govern our private rights. However, putting the concerns of others ahead of ourselves is very unsettling to citizens today. Too often, America is no longer a polite society. We are competitive to the point of being rude; we are self-centered to the level of crudeness. We observe these tendencies all around us in millions of personal interactions in business, traffic, recreation, social settings, etc. Therefore, **GREATNESS** in our personal lives is buried under our pursuits of unwise, personal freedoms.

At one time, all of society was governed by the Ten Commandments. Not so now, we require tens of millions of laws to attempt the same level of social cooperation and still American culture is rife with selfishness. We must change our behaviors.

Public policy by definition guides and restricts our personal behaviors. Traffic laws are written to permit the maximum number of drivers to use the roadways to arrive safely and efficiently at their destinations. Stop signs, speed limits, and rights of way govern the way we drive and are necessary in society. Similarly, public policy restricts our personal freedoms for the common good. This same rationale is applied to all aspects of social interaction. In childhood, principles of right living are taught to us at home by parents, such as how to obey instructions, how to speak to others, and how to share our space and rights with others. More good behaviors are taught in schools: how to line up, when to be quiet and listen, and what to do and not do in public. Other public policies are taught to us by government, such as how to comply with contracts, how to be fair with financial transactions, and where the rights of the individual stop and the rights of society begin.

In America, our founding fathers decided that our nation would be created around the justice taught in the Bible or the Judeo-Christian standards of right and wrong. Right was not defined by the wishes of a king or even dictated by a class of people. Right was defined by the Golden Rule of doing unto others as we want them to do unto us. Morals were characterized by modesty, faithfulness, and self-restraint. At one time in America, civility or common courtesy was assumed and this code was founded in the morality taught in the Bible.

Americans need not be ashamed of our origin nor should we change our foundation. In the Bible, we are exhorted to be wise, sober, and self-controlled. We are exhorted to work hard, care for others, raise a godly family, and live under the law. ***The wise attention to morality is America's foundation.*** The Bible refers to its teaching as wisdom and rejection of its teaching as foolishness. The founding fathers, just like you and me, had difficulty living consistently with the standards of the Bible. But we must renew our pledge to live wisely, responsibly, and with integrity or the alternative will be the loss of freedom due to our foolish decision making. As noted earlier, our values determine our decisions. If we lose our values, we lose our compass and rudder. We will be like a balloon in the sky floating whichever direction the hot air blows us, even if into a cactus.

Biblical wisdom requires no improvement or updating. Wisdom is the practical application of moral principles. We can no longer simply argue, "The Bible says" as our basis of thought and behavior. Biblical authority should be enough, but our society no longer respects the authority of the Bible. However, we can reason from the logic and morality of the Scriptures to defend, illustrate, and prove that *wisdom is healthier than foolishness* and that *principled living produces more freedom* than uncontrolled living.

Just as Bo illustrated that learning the principle of cleanliness in our home gained him the freedom to live inside our home. The values taught in the Bible and demonstrated to us in Jesus Christ are the principles that will regain *GREATNESS* in our nation today.

Remember the magic: *The magic for America is that free and moral men and women produce devoted families, prosperous businesses, and peaceful communities*. There is no other magic, no other design, and no other way for America. Free and moral citizens will produce a great and productive nation.

Chapter *22*

Who Is The Alpha Dog?

My search for my next canine companion is just beginning. I want a working dog with strong character and great loyalty. I want the power of Foxworth, my Newfie, and the devotion of Max, my Rottie. I loved them both, and now they are gone. I cannot replace these special dogs, but I will add to their number another friend with whom to walk and confide. A good dog is not man's best friend, but he is a great friend.

As I study different breeds, I come upon this line in characterization of the larger dogs, "needs a strong leader who establishes himself as the 'alpha' dog in the family or this dog will dominate." I like the traits in a dog of strength, determination, power, and grace. However, enjoying a strong-willed dog requires an alpha to teach him obedience. Leadership is essential in a family; a loving, unselfish, kind, and principled leader is healthy for a family.

The question is: Who is the alpha dog over America and over the entire human family? Generation after generation, century after century, is there a virtuous leader for people to follow? Or are we to set our own rules, establish our own morality, and prioritize our own values?

The Bible answers that question with crystal clarity, "No." For example, Job in the Old Testament is overrun with hardships, the loss of most of his wealth, the death of his children, their spouses and their children, and finally his body is struck with pain and disfigurement. Job was never given the answer about why these disasters occurred. As Bible students, we are told more than Job was. Actually, it was Satan behind these trials. But in the last chapters of the book, God speaks to Job in a series of statements and rhetorical questions which can be paraphrased with this question, "Who is the Alpha dog, Job? Are you?" Job is convicted of his prideful independence in questioning God's purposes and writes this, *"I have heard of you by the hearing of the ear but now my eye sees you; therefore I despise myself and repent in dust and ashes."* (Job 42: 5, 6)

Job was finally admitting that **God is in charge**; God does as His purposes dictate. The living God is the not only the Alpha but also the Omega. He is the beginning of all of life and He is the conclusion of life. God is the only God. Job was written to illustrate this truth: God deserves our respect and obedience. Job is another example of a virtuous individual receiving dignity, honor, and blessing. The final verses in Job read "And the Lord blessed the latter days of Job more than his beginning." (Job 42:12)

The Bible makes one consistent and repetitive statement regarding our relationship to God. *We are accountable to God*. We are His highest creation on the earth, we have proven to be rebellious subjects, and yet we are the objects of His love. His love can be defined as God's heartfelt and devoted commitment to our highest good. We are walking away from Him when we disobey, disregard, and reject His authority. Our unworthy behavior does not change His love; but our sinfulness in disobeying God's rules separates us from His goodness and leaves us to suffer judgment.

As a nation, the United States is accountable to God. As individuals, we are accountable to God. He is the Alpha over the family of the human race. His leadership over our nation and over our lives can be the most rewarding and peaceful state. Jesus called the life He came to provide "the abundant life."

In fact, living in harmony with God is our happiest state of being. **Submission to God is joyful, fulfilling, hopeful, and eternal.** Not to submit to Him is wasteful, unhealthy, and frustrating.

God is in the full-time business of calling the entire human race back from its sinfulness and rebellion. His Son, Jesus Christ, is our Savior and God's sacrifice for our sins. God placed the penalty for our sin onto Jesus and when He died on that awful cross, the penalty for man's sinfulness and rebellion was paid in full. All of us can be restored to a right relationship to God through a confession of our sin and by opening our lives to God through faith in Jesus Christ. We can accept His authority, His verdict over us as guilty, and His loving forgiveness through a simple prayer of faith: *"Lord Jesus, I need and want You as my Savior to forgive my sinfulness and to be the Master for my life. I accept your love, grace, and authority over my life."* Individuals of every societal station and lifestyle must pray this prayer. As individuals, we pray for personal salvation. As a nation, America can be rescued from our national moral crisis.

We, the people, must confess our rebellion and accept Jesus as our Savior and Master. No other way for personal salvation or the prosperous, peaceful future of our nation exists.

The essential truth is this: ***W—O—W—A*** can point us in the right, practical direction of ***GREATNESS***. The U.S. Constitution or amendments to the Constitution might be helpful, but these steps alone will not return America to ***GREATNESS***. Better politicians and policies might improve our way of life, but ultimately, ***our relationship to God is the foundation that will make America great***.

GREATNESS is not measured in what you and I have or do but in living a life in right relationship to God Almighty and to each other.

The next debate of any consequence to our future in America will be: ***What values will shape America?*** Only two possible choices exist: Will Americans pursue God's favor or will we continue to pursue self-gratification?

We pledge allegiance to America for which our flag stands, *one Nation under God, indivisible, with liberty and justice for all*. God requires a higher moral standard for the USA because of the wealth, freedom, and security He has given to our nation. This pledge demands noble, personal values: ***W—O—W—A***.

Celebrate the magic: ***The magic for America is that free and moral men and women produce devoted families, prosperous businesses, and peaceful communities***.

"But he who is noble plans noble things,
And on noble things he stands."
Isaiah 32:8

Can we trust each other and our government to make decisions formed by our shared, noble values?

The obvious answer is that we don't, and sadly we can't, trust one another. Why? Decisions on all levels from personal to national are no longer made on the basis of honorable values. We may call it pragmatism or compassion or self-centeredness, but we are living in a mis-directed culture. We can do better. We must do better. God, help us to do better, we pray.

Franklin D. Roosevelt defined freedom in America as freedom of speech and of worship coupled with freedom from want and fear. Quite differently, Ronald Reagan defined America's freedom as freedom of expression, religion, and enterprise. Either way, freedom demands a population that upholds collectively certain national principles, priorities, and values. These values at one time formed a core within America. This moral core is fundamental to our nation. This moral core can answer the questions that presently are kicking America's backside.

It is not enough to complain, we must become reformers.
It is not enough to shout "Fire," we must provide the water hose.

It is not enough to think we're right, we must win the debate.

W—O—W—A does all this, when we act on principle.

Chapter 23

To Those Who Disagree, I Say.

I am asked two questions by my fellow Christians. The first is: *Considering the moral decline in America, is there hope for America?* The short answer is "Absolutely yes!"

My answer is not based on the nightly news or the continuous commentary on the news, either those from a conservative bent or from the liberal side. I watch and read both perspectives nationally and locally.

My answer is from Romans 1:16 which says: "For I am not ashamed of the gospel, for it is the power of God for salvation to everyone who believes . . . ." The good news from God is that He is still in the business of forgiving sin, even mine, and creating new lives, new values, and new relationships for anyone who turns from sin and turns to Jesus. My hope is in Jesus. I am not discouraged by the opposition to righteousness or by the stubbornness of self-righteousness.

After all, God changed me. I do not ask you to follow me except in the sense that I am following Christ. I do not have the answers, but I do know and pray to the God who does know all the questions and the answers.

The second question is: *Should we care what happens to America?* After all, America does not seem to be in biblical prophecy and certainly America has not always acted morally. Perhaps God is judging America.

Again, I point to the Bible: "For God so loved the world, that He gave His Son. . . . ." We are not in the position to say when God stops saving men and women or even reviving whole cities; Jonah and Nineveh come to mind. Nations are God's creation even as families are. Most certainly, God will measure America according to His righteousness, but until that final judgment occurs we are standing with Him as long as we are praying for and laboring in the work of the Gospel.

America has failed God; I have failed Him too. Thankfully, God's love does not stop when we fail Him morally. God's love is both longsuffering and patient. God in Jesus Christ is forgiving. I am eternally thankful for His forgiveness in my life.

The ideal called America is being tested. We began this discussion thinking of America as a grand experiment in human relations. I believe and our fore-fathers believed that we, Americans, are God's handiwork; He entrusted us with immense freedom, a democratic form of government, and incredible natural and human resources. The test is: Will we use our freedom for **GREATNESS** or misuse it for dishonor? Currently, we are misusing and twisting America into a secular society, a post-Christian culture.

America was designed as a constitutional, democratic republic founded on Judeo-Christian principles. Sadly, we are turning from God, corrupting the moral foundation of our nation, and losing the ideals that make America's freedoms possible and sustainable.

The U.S. Constitution has failed us. Or, has the American citizenry failed to maintain the values that our democratic republic requires? It is time to stop competing over political majorities in power and haranguing over legislative tricks to frustrate the power of the opposition. It is time to present a fresh, revitalizing vision of noble values. This presentation can be gloriously uplifting and deliciously nutritious. We can paint a picture of integrity, ambition, generosity, compassion, and unity. We can create a scene of national brotherhood, individual nobility, and neighborhood friendship. It is time to illustrate just how great Americans and America can be while enjoying a contagious excitement of right living. Can you be that righteous artist who can inspire, lead, and work with others? Heroes don't just curse at the darkness; heroes find solutions, build consensus, and inspire men and women of all ages to **GREATNESS**.

We return to the original question: ***Can free men and women govern themselves especially over the long term?***

Let the conversation begin!

Chapter 24

Greatness Is . . .

Greatness is for everyone. Because God is for everyone. God created each one for the greatness that He has designed. No, I may not be a great baseball player, or a Broadway performer, or a Nobel Prize winner. I may not reach every goal that I want to reach. But I can be everything God has designed me to be and in doing so I can please God, please myself, and please a great many people along life's way. I may even surprise myself and others at how well I have done.

The promise of God is ***"Blessed is the nation whose God is the Lord."*** (Psalms 33:12)

The corollary is blessed or happy is the man and woman, boy and girl, teenager, and old person whose God is the Lord. Greatness is directly related to the god in each individual life. Entire nations are blessed by God Almighty by choosing to make the LORD God in life.

However, many deceivers and counterfeits lurk through our everyday lives. These deceivers shout their lies; some of which are:

1. God isn't concerned with your happiness. He takes away pleasure from life.
2. Many roads can lead to prosperity. Pick the one that suits you.
3. You have a right to be happy. Someone will or should give it to you.
4. Religion and spiritual disciplines will fulfill your life. Find your own path.
5. Lucky people are the ones who find fulfillment in life. Buy a lottery ticket.

Unfortunately, many more charlatans boast of their paths to happiness. Don't be mistaken. The truth is that fulfillment is found in a relationship with God and Him alone through faith in Jesus Christ.

The truth is that God created us for pleasure. We can bring to Him pleasure and He can bring pleasure to mankind. The pursuit of pleasure is entirely natural. God gives to us beauty to behold, aromas to savor, textures to appreciate, and spices to relish. God gave to us a world full of pleasure. He gave us sexual pleasure with which to consummate marriage, intellectual puzzles to unravel, physical challenges to test us, and emotional feelings to enhance every experience. God's plan is for our highest pleasure not the cheap thrills of over-indulgence.

The mountaintop experience of pleasure is the spiritual enjoyment of fellowship with God Himself. As with all pleasures, the more effort, training, and experience we gain with obtaining this pleasure the higher our enjoyment of each God created delicacy. I could cook a steak but a chef would create a feast. I might smell a flower but a perfumer would create a fragrance. And so on, genuine and lifelong enjoyment must be pursued with skill and practice under the guidelines and values designed by God, the Creator.

Physics, biology, and mathematics display truth. Mankind did not put truth there. God did. Man cannot make his own truth or design his own laws. Scientists discover the laws that are already written and work within those laws. Newton did not create gravity. He discovered it, studied it, and wrote about it. Scientists since Newton have learned to make use of gravity in architecture and how to overcome it in space travel but gravity will not and cannot be negated or ignored. The laws of God are immutable regardless of our efforts.

The very same laws are encoded in man's soul. The moral conscience, the body's immune systems, and the very blood pulsing through our veins are God's laws written inside each person. Man can and should discover them and utilize them, however, when man tries to ignore them, change them, or nullify them, then we do so as inviting trouble. Just like the man who drives while being intoxicated or cleans a loaded gun, mankind must respect the laws or truths that God has given us for our protection.

The laws of God guide us toward maximizing pleasures and protect us from abusing the pleasures He has provided. We can enjoy the sunset but we must keep an eye on the road. We should enjoy a well prepared meal but we must not enjoy them too much or too often. Our stomachs will tell us when to stop. These same laws written by God are NOT fabrications of cultures or of religions. The moral laws are from God with the purpose of maximizing pleasures for a lifetime.

The Bible says that *the blessing of the LORD makes rich, and he adds no sorrow with it.* Can we say the same thing regarding all the counterfeit blessings around us? Will all the deceitful promises that evil makes to us bring fulfillment? Can these lies be trusted to add no sorrow? These lies come to us with beautiful bows and fancy colored papers. They can seem convincing but do these promises parallel the commands and blessings of God. The commands of God are not arbitrary and there is no other way.

I suggest individually and nationally, we decide now to pursue God given pleasures in God commanded paths. I beg each of us to accept His way as my way and our way.

The ultimate pleasure is life in pursuit of God.

The supreme goal is knowledge of God.

The eternal reward is communion with God.

The greatest success is pleasing God.

GREATNESS is for everyone but it is not found on every path.

Proverbs 4:18, 19 reads:

"But the path of the righteous is like the light of dawn, which shines brighter and brighter until full day. The way of the wicked is like deep darkness; they do not know over what they stumble."

The magic for America is that <u>free</u> and <u>moral</u> men and women produce devoted families, prosperous businesses, and peaceful communities. We can govern ourselves when we live by the American values of *WORK, OTHERS, WEALTH,* and *AUTHORITY.*

Statement of Shared Values

We thank you, God, for the endless blessings of freedom and we joyfully assume responsibility for maintaining our freedom.

We hereby affirm these statements of shared responsibilities.

*Our government must never promise to do for us what we must do for ourselves. And, we must never ask our government to give to us what we must earn through **work**.*

*Our nation was commissioned by God to protect and enable the rights of everyone in a concerned and compassionate community. Our personal worth is found in serving **others**.*

*Our relationships and our personal character traits are the measures of real and lasting **wealth**. Family is our greatest asset and our most important gift to the future.*

*Our peaceful society depends on the adherence by all to the laws of the land. If the law is to be changed, it is through public debate and submission to divine **authority**.*

Therefore, we believe that freedom is an earned right. <u>This right can be lost if not honored and upheld.</u> The responsibility is mine.

Author's Personal Information

I am an unashamed lover of my country, the United States of America. From my teenage years, I have wanted to serve my country and make life in America better for myself and for the next generation. Life, as they say, got in the way, and what I thought might be a life in the military or in politics or even in religion became forty years of marriage, earning a living, raising children, and keeping busy. I have loved it, and thank God for my life. I worked as an automobile and truck technician, started and managed three repair shops, and I went to many school activities.

Forty years later, I am still happily married with seven grandchildren, and I teach diesel technology in a community college. My desire to serve my nation has morphed into a message that I believe should be considered by all Americans. I want to say something to America, all of America.

The message is be careful. Our nation is being tested by the freedoms we embrace. Freedom to choose can become freedom to rewrite our American way of life in unhealthy ways.

Personal signifi cance and the growth into greatness is a path our forbearers wanted for every citizen of America. Life, liberty, and the pursuit of happiness is a goal to which each generation of Americans must aspire. This worthy goal has not been reached by most nations now or in the past. Likewise, not every generation in America has lived up to the responsibilities of liberty and justice for all. Now time has given to me and you our turn at the controls of our individual lives and our united life.

Can we govern ourselves rightly? We will observe the signifi cance of each other and gain the greatness that is ours to grasp. Will I help my neighbor and will he help me? Can I feel good about myself, my family, my work, and my community? How will my freedom build a better place for the next generation?

I challenge myself and every American to aspire to greatness. Greatness is for everyone! I believe that; this is our God-given ambition. Four traits of greatness are not steps of selfhelp; rather, these traits are the headlights pointing us into our future.